102 ___ 442 2

D1338847

Observin

Retu
Fine

This book is dedicated to the memory
of Niko Tinbergen
(1907–1988)

Observing Animal Behaviour

Design and analysis of quantitative data

Marian Stamp Dawkins

Mary Snow Fellow in Biological Sciences
Somerville College
Oxford

and

Animal Behaviour Research Group
Department of Zoology
University of Oxford

OXFORD
UNIVERSITY PRESS

OXFORD
UNIVERSITY PRESS

Great Clarendon Street, Oxford OX2 6DP

Oxford University Press is a department of the University of Oxford.
It furthers the University's objective of excellence in research, scholarship,
and education by publishing worldwide in

Oxford New York

Auckland Cape Town Dar es Salaam Hong Kong Karachi
Kuala Lumpur Madrid Melbourne Mexico City Nairobi
New Delhi Shanghai Taipei Toronto
With offices in
Argentina Austria Brazil Chile Czech Republic France Greece
Guatemala Hungary Italy Japan South Korea Poland Portugal
Singapore Switzerland Thailand Turkey Ukraine Vietnam

Oxford is a registered trade mark of Oxford University Press
in the UK and in certain other countries

Published in the United States
by Oxford University Press Inc., New York

ISBN 978-0-19-856936-7

Printed in the United Kingdom by
Lightning Source UK Ltd., Milton Keynes

Contents

Preface

There are several different reasons for writing a book on observing animal behaviour. The first reason (the one that drove me, with a considerable degree of frustration, to think about writing this book in the first place) is the tendency of students and colleagues to ignore the observational phase of a behavioural study and go straight into designing complex experiments without really understanding their animals at all. This often leads them to overlook important aspects of the behaviour of a species, sometimes to design completely inappropriate or impractical experiments, and then to be frustrated when the experiment doesn't 'work'. This book aims to show that a little time spent observing goes a long way to improving research, even if it may also, in the end, involve experimentation.

The second reason grew out of my own interest in animal welfare, particularly that of farm animals. There is a great deal of interest in the welfare of animals in zoos, on farms and in the wild, all places where experiments may not be possible or ethically desirable. This is where observation really comes into its own, particularly where it is systematic and done on a large scale. Animals can be studied '*in situ*', in the place a where they live, and so any results are directly applicable to those situations. The replication needed for statistical analysis can often be achieved by combining data from different sources, giving a picture of the 'real world' that tightly controlled experiments in one place cannot do. The potential of observation as a non-invasive research tool has not yet been fully appreciated and one of the aims of the book is to show people just what can be accomplished without the need for any sort of experimental manipulation.

This leads to a third reason for an interest in observation. The advent of CCTV, video, GPS tracking and other devices that can be installed in farms, zoos, and even on wild animals themselves, now allows us to study the behaviour of undisturbed animals in places where we could not previously follow them and for longer and in more detail than was ever possible before. No longer does observation just mean that which can be collected with pen and paper (although pen and paper still hold an honourable place in behavioural observation). Observation—taken broadly to include the new technology—has an immense potential in the study of behaviour. The aim of this book is therefore to introduce students (and others) to the power of observation, starting with simple and easily accessible methods suitable for student projects, but opening their eyes to the possibilities that now exist for much more sophisticated analysis of observational data. It aims to show that observational techniques are not the poor relation of experiment but hugely important and informative in their own right.

I should perhaps say what this book is not. It is not a statistics textbook, although I would like to think that at least some readers will come to a better understanding of what statistics is all about in a very painless way through reading about animal behaviour. It should be read alongside one of the excellent introductory books on statistics that are now available, such Grafen and Hails' *Modern Statistics for the Life Sciences* (2002). Nor is it intended as a comprehensive account of methodology in behavioural research. Martin and Bateson's *Measuring Behaviour* (1993) and Paul Lehner's *Handbook of Ethological Methods* (1996) both go into considerably more detail on techniques, methods, and different experimental designs and should be consulted for a more advanced treatment of topics covered here. Bonnie Ploger and Ken Yasukawa's *Exploring Animal Behavior in Laboratory and Field* (2003) provides many more specific examples and ideas for actual projects. This book's role is as a companion, a guide to the study of animal behaviour. It is primarily intended for students doing undertaking their first research project but I hope it will also be useful to anyone who as ever been fascinated by animal behaviour and wanted to know how to study it further. It stresses the supreme importance of asking the right questions but does not pretend to give a detailed list of all the answers. On the contrary, it aims to get people to think for themselves about what the whole process of doing research is all about and how they might go about finding their own answers in one of the most absorbing areas in the whole of biology. It emphasizes observation rather than experimentation, but observation that has gone beyond 'just' watching to a science in its own right.

I would like to thank Robin McCleery and two anonymous referees for their helpful comments on an early draft of the manuscript. Generous friends and colleagues allowed me to use their wonderful photographs. SBC provided inspiration I could not have done without.

1 The power of observation

Imagine it is a bright sunny day and that you are sitting on the wall of a harbour with your back leaning against a warm stone wall, idly watching some gulls poking around in the sandy mud below you. The sun glances off the sea in the distance and even the mud, left wet and glistening by the ebbing tide, has a beauty of its own. The warmth of the wall against your body and the sun on your face are soporific and you are almost half asleep when you are suddenly jolted out of your reverie by the most extraordinary sight. The gull nearest to you is paddling its feet rapidly up and down as it if were running furiously on the spot. As you watch, you realise that this high speed pummelling takes it ever so slightly backwards and that every few seconds it pauses, pecks the mud and apparently finds something to eat. What on earth can it be doing? And it is not just one gull. Several others are taking up the same peculiar behaviour and there are splashy noises made by pairs of vibrating webbed feet all round you. Why? What makes them do it? What do they get out of it? Why haven't you seen this behaviour before? Is there something special about this day or this state of the tide? Are they following each other's example? Does it really help them to find food? If so, how?

Your idle reverie is now shattered. Your apparently casual observations could be about turn to you into a detective and set you on the trail of asking some very illuminating questions about the behaviour of animals. However, while it is obvious that your observations of what animals do has led you to *ask* questions about their behaviour, it may be less obvious that further observations, ideally more systematic and quantitative than your original ones, are also crucial to finding the answers.

1.1 Testing hypotheses

Many people make the mistake of thinking that science just means performing experiments, as though you couldn't get anywhere, at least not anywhere scientifically respectable, without actively manipulating the world in some way. But this is to misunderstand what science is really about. The essence of science is acquiring knowledge through testing hypotheses. Setting up a controlled experiment—in other words attempting to manipulate the outcome and make things happen when and where you want them to—is certainly one way of demonstrating the accuracy of a hypothesis and its predictions, but it is not the only way. Predictions can also be tested very powerfully by pitting them against future observations as they unfold naturally, with no intervention on anyone's part. For example, astronomers who make precise predictions about the appearance of a comet and specify the year, month, day, and even the exact hour when you will be able to see it have not done, indeed could not do, an experiment. But, provided the comet does appear when expected, no-one is going to accuse them of being unscientific. On the contrary, the very fact that they are able to make such precise predictions about the future convinces us that they have a very profound understanding of the way the solar system works.

This book is about how we can do much the same thing in the study of animal behaviour. It is about how we can start by watching what animals do and wondering how and why they do it, move on to formulating theories about what is going on, and then test them using further observation—but this time more systematically and quantitatively than with the casual kind of observation with which we began. It is about the scientific study of animal behaviour that can be done, at least initially, without experiment, and is therefore particularly suitable for studies of the undisturbed behaviour of animals in their natural environments or in situations where experimental manipulation is impractical, undesirable, or even seen as unethical. It is written primarily for people wanting to undertake their first systematic study of animal behaviour, such as students doing a research project, but I hope it will also be of use to anyone whose interest has ever been caught by watching what animals do and has wanted to find out more. I particularly hope it will be useful to people who study wild animals, or animals on farms or zoos, or indeed anywhere where the chosen method of study is '*in situ*'— that is, in the place where the animals live—and where any sort of intervention is difficult or likely to detract from the validity of the results.

1.2   Experiment and observation

To avoid confusion, I shall use the term 'experiment' in its most commonly used sense of a deliberate manipulation where a researcher makes some intervention or interference to test a hypothesis, and the term 'observation' where the researcher makes no attempt to control events (as with the appearance of a comet) but simply observes what happens. This is sometimes called a natural experiment. From a scientific viewpoint, both are 'experiments', since all this word really means is 'a test', but the distinction—intervention versus letting things happen—is critical to this book and I shall generally use the shorthand 'experiment' v. 'observation' rather than the more cumbersome 'manipulative experiment' v. 'natural experiment'.

Fortunately, we in the behavioural sciences are not alone in wanting to make full use of observation: not only astronomers, but geologists studying earthquakes and volcanoes, physicists studying the origins of the Universe, and medical epidemiologists trying to understand the causes and spread of diseases, also rely heavily on statistical or mathematical, but non-experimental, techniques to reach their conclusions. We can borrow some of their methods and combine them with the long tradition of observation that goes back to Niko Tinbergen and Konrad Lorenz, sometimes called the founding fathers of the study of animal behaviour. The result, as we will see, is a powerful mix of the scientific and the natural—a statistical approach grounded in what real animals do.

To see how this might work in practice, let us go back to the scene at the harbour. Rest and relaxation are now impossible. You decide you want to try and find some scientific answers to your questions. What should you do next?

1.3   Different kinds of question

Although you may not have realized it, the questions that arose as you watched the gulls were of several different types, each demanding a rather different sort of answer. The questions 'Why?' and 'What do they get out of it?', for example, are asking about the function of the behaviour—that is, what evolutionary advantage gulls gain by paddling their feet up and down. Why would natural selection favour gulls that did this behaviour over those that did not? You might start wondering whether the action of the gulls' feet had some effect on the consistency of the mud that made it easier for them to see or catch their food. This might set you on the path of making more specific observations, such as exactly how fast the gulls moved their feet, to see whether this was consistent with what is known about the physics of mud. You might need to record the behaviour on video so that you could measure the foot movements accurately, and this, too, would be a form of observation—technology-aided observation certainly, but still observation of what the gulls were doing without interference.

Niko Tinbergen (1963), who did almost more than anyone else to promote the scientific study of animal behaviour, called this kind of question a 'survival value' question, meaning that what we really want to know is how the behaviour makes the animal more likely to survive. These days, we would probably add 'and reproduce' and even 'and help the reproduction of kin' because evolution is not just about adult survival but about passing genes on to the next generation. Such questions are now called, more comprehensively, questions about *adaptation*. Survival value or adaptation questions are not, however, the only ones you could ask about foot paddling. You can also ask 'what makes gulls do it?', 'why do they start?', or 'what stimulates them?' These are questions about the immediate *causation* of behaviour and they call for answers of a rather different kind. Gulls don't foot-paddle all the time and they don't do it on hard surfaces. So what makes them do it at all? Is it particular weather conditions? Particular states of the tide? Or even particular kinds of mud? They might also be copying each other, so that part of the 'cause' would be the sight of the other gulls doing the same behaviour. You could begin to answer such questions by making detailed observations of exactly when and where you saw foot-paddling happening and whether foot-paddling in one gull is followed by its neighbours all doing the same thing. In later chapters, you will learn how to use your observations to answer such questions.

Another kind of question might also occur to you about the gulls, about how their behaviour *develops*. Do they have to learn to foot-paddle? Do gull chicks hatch with the behaviour fully formed or do they perhaps perfect it with experience? A comparison between older and younger gulls might be very instructive here. Do the younger ones do it in the same way? Do they obtain as much food? As we will see later, observational studies can be very successfully used to answer questions about the development of behaviour in young animals, particularly where individuals can be recognized and studied over crucial periods in their lives, such as when they are being weaned or separated from their parents.

1.4   Why observation is important

Throughout this book we will see the crucial role that observation plays in answering all sorts of questions about animal behaviour, sometimes as a prelude to doing experiments, but sometimes as a powerful tool in its own right that can replace experiments altogether. Experiments, we should never forget, have costs: costs in money, time and equipment, and often also to the animals. By carrying out an observational study first, and really understanding the behaviour of your animals, you can cut down on all of these costs and enormously increase the likely success of any experiments you do subsequently. For example, Dorothy Cheney and Robert Seyfarth (1990) carried out a pioneering series of field experiments with free-living vervet monkeys (*Cercopithecus aethiops*) in the Amboseli National Park in Kenya (Fig. 1.1). They were able to show that the monkeys had different alarm calls for

Fig. 1.1   A group of vervet monkeys (*Photograph by Dorothy Cheney*).

different types of predators—a primitive vocabulary for telling each other what sort of danger they were in. There was one kind of alarm call a monkey gave when it had spotted a leopard that caused the other monkeys to rush up a tree, the safest thing to do when a leopard is around. A quite different alarm call was given to a martial eagle overhead and this caused the other monkeys to hide in bushes, while a third kind of alarm call, the snake alarm call, caused them to stand on their hind legs and peer into the grass. The calls were quite distinct even to the human ear and the responses of the other monkeys were quite different too.

Now, in order to show that the monkeys were really responding to these different alarm calls as opposed to just seeing the predators for themselves, Cheney and Seyfarth conducted experiments in which they hid a tape recorder in the long grass near where the monkeys were feeding and then broadcast either the snake or the eagle or the leopard alarm calls. They showed that the monkeys immediately responded in the appropriate way (peering into grass, heading for bushes, or running up a tree) to the sounds they heard even though there were no predators around. It was of course the experiments that convinced everybody that the monkeys knew what the sounds meant, but it was the fact that there had been long periods of observation before any experiments were attempted that made the experiments, when they were done, so successful.

The experiments themselves took a long time. Tape recorders and loud speakers had to be moved around the Park and set up in the grass without disturbing the monkeys. There could then be a long wait until the right moment came to play the sounds. This of course had to be done over and over again to achieve results that were statistically significant. Cheney and Seyfarth had, therefore, to be sure before they embarked on the study that it was going to be worth doing. And they were convinced that it would be an exciting experiment to do precisely because they had already spent a long time observing the monkeys and noting, over and over again, the ways in which they responded to the calls of other monkeys. Their experiments, when they did them, were therefore very targeted and carefully planned to test a specific hypothesis about how monkeys should behave in different situations. That hypothesis had not come out of nowhere. It had come from their many hours of watching vervet monkeys in the field. They had already developed a strong hunch that the different alarm calls meant different things to those monkeys, and it was therefore clear to them that the next step was to do an experimental test. Observations had thus paved the way for the experiments.

Sometimes observations can be so dramatic in their own right that they make experiments almost unnecessary. Jane Goodall (1968) (see Fig. 1.2) observed chimpanzees using twigs to extract termites from their mounds. She watched as a chimpanzee would poke a stick into a mound, wait until the insects crawled up the stick, then pull it out and eat the termites. She even observed chimpanzees prepare their tools by stripping leaves off them so that

Fig. 1.2   Jane Goodall observing chimpanzees at the Gombe Stream Reserve. Dr. Jane Goodall, DBE, Founder, Jane Goodall Institute, UN Messenger of Peace: www.janegoodall.org

they would fit better into the entrance to the mound. No-one had reported such behaviour before and her observations changed our view of what chimpanzees are capable of doing. No longer were we the only tool-using or even the only tool-making ape. Our ideas of what it is to be human were changed by what animals were observed to be doing in the wild.

1.5 The limits of observation

While I shall be stressing the value of observation throughout this book, it is certainly not my intention to argue against experiments altogether or to imply that they are never necessary. Despite all my emphasis on observation, experiment is still the king of scientific method. It is the only way in which we can convincingly separate correlation from causation. Observation only shows us what correlates with what—that is, how the behaviour of animals consistently varies with some other factor such as the time of day, or how long since they have eaten, or how close they are to another animal. These correlations suggest hypotheses about what might cause the behaviour but they do not conclusively show cause and effect. Taken at face value, they can be very misleading. For example, Moehlman (1979) found a clear correlation between the number of juvenile 'helpers' and the number of pups raised by black-backed jackals (*Canis mesomelas*). These monogamous and highly sociable dogs live in groups that consist of a breeding pair and the young from previous years. The young jackals often stay with their parents for a year or so and help to rear their younger brothers and sisters. They guard them and bring them food and play with them. Moehlman's results appeared to show that having more helpers enabled the parents to rear more pups, with up to six pups surviving as long as they had help from two to three juveniles (Fig. 1.3).

But the correlation in this case did not necessarily indicate causation. The parents that had two or three helpers were also—of necessity—older than those that had one or none at all. Younger parents, particularly ones breeding for the first time, had simply not had time to accumulate any juvenile helpers, and so the graph shown in Fig. 1.3 might in reality be showing a correlation between breeding success and the age of the parents. It is thus not clear why (causally) some parents were more successful at producing surviving offspring than others. It could have been because they had more helpers, but it might also have been for other reasons such as parental age, or parental experience, or just because they were occupying a better den site than the others. Relying on just that particular correlation does not enable us to say which of those factors, if any, was causing the variation in pup survival.

Such ambiguities in identifying causal connections from observational data are precisely what have lead many people to believe that experiments are

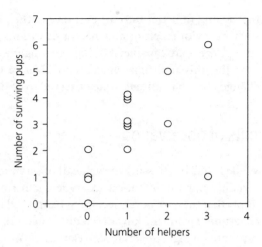

Fig. 1.3   Jackal pups are more likely to survive the more helpers their parents have (from Moehlman, 1979).

essential in all scientific investigations. Only experimental manipulation, they will argue, will allow a separation of causation from correlation: it is essential to do experiments in which everything is properly controlled and just one or a few variables at a time are manipulated. Only if we can control when and where something happens by manipulating the proposed cause will we ever be able to sort out true cause from misleading correlation.

While not in any way disputing the importance of experiment as the 'gold standard' in revealing causal pathways, it is important to point out that there many areas of science where high levels of experimental control are not possible or even desirable. We have already mentioned astronomy and geology as two examples. Many areas of medicine and human health, such as the study of diet or life style, also suffer from ethical or other constraints on what can or cannot be controlled experimentally. Animal behaviour is another such field. The difficulties we sometimes have with experimentally controlling everything in an animal's environment do not make it unscientific. It just means that we have to approach the problem of disentangling correlation and causation in more subtle (and often more statistical) ways.

An experimental approach to understanding the causal connections between helpers and pup survival in jackals, for example, would be to make sure that parents of all ages had the same numbers of helpers and an equal chance of getting a good den site. But just imagine what would happen if we tried to impose such a regime on wild jackals in the interests of good experimental design. We would have to randomly assign pairs of jackals to different dens, which might mean moving them out of a den they had chosen for themselves. We would have to forcibly remove some helpers from older parents and give them to younger parents even though they might be total strangers. The result would be chaos. The animals would be disturbed, their behaviour unnatural and the experiment, although superficially 'controlled', would be totally useless as far as telling us anything meaningful about the natural behaviour of jackals was concerned.

No, we need different approaches, approaches that allow us to study the behaviour of undisturbed animals and still allow us to avoid confusing causation with correlation. Fortunately, we can borrow from other sciences and we can develop methods of our own. In the course of this book we will see just how far those approaches can take us and what wonderful rewards there are from observational and non-interventionist approaches that stop short of experiment. We will see that even if we cannot control our animals as precisely as an experimentalist would like us to, we can, as Schneirla (1950) and Altmann (1974) put it, control ourselves. We can design our observations with as much care for disentangling cause from correlation as any experimentalist. We can choose when and what and how long to observe and that gives us, as we will see, almost as much power in making deductions from our data as in a controlled experiment. We also have the added benefit of knowing that we have only minimally disturbed the animals and have studied their natural behaviour. Although experiment may be king, observation is its general in the field, its link with the real world, its supplier of hypotheses and, in its own way, a tester of those hypotheses too. This, rather than doing away with experiments altogether, will be the message of this book.

1.6   New ways of observing

With modern technology, observation in its broadest sense of non-interventionist, non-experimental data collection assumes an even greater significance. Equipped with video, tracking systems, and other methods of remote recording, the general in the field can 'observe' behaviour and send information back to headquarters in ways that we are only just beginning to appreciate.

Iain Douglas Hamilton and his team, for example, put GPS trackers onto bull elephants (Fig. 1.4) and found that, contrary to what had been thought, so-called lone bulls appeared to be constantly in communication with other males and were coordinating their behaviour with them. Although they kept their distance from each other and appeared to be moving independently, the movements of the various males suggested that they were part of a huge, spread out network. Tracks from the different males followed each other so closely that they appeared to be bound by an invisible thread. When one

Fig. 1.4   A bull elephant 'Boone' wearing a GPS collar. Photograph by Iain Douglas-Hamilton.

moved, the other did too, even though they might be some distance from each other. It also became apparent that the elephants could distinguish between areas where they were protected from humans and 'corridors' between protected areas. The GPS trackers indicated that the elephants spent longer, and moved more slowly, in the protected areas and moved quickly through the unprotected areas in between (Douglas-Hamilton et al., 2005).

This kind of observation and the insights that it gives us into the secret behaviour of animals has only become possible with the availability of new techniques. Together with computers that can help us deal with large amounts of data, video, GPS trackers, and other remote sensors have given a whole new meaning to 'observation.' No longer are we confined to what we can write down on paper or punch into a keyboard. Observation now demands just as much sophisticated analysis as experimentation itself, and sometimes even more.

1.7   Observation and the '3Rs'

As we have seen, the power of the experimental approach is that it systematically severs the connections between two events and allows us to manipulate the world to see which ones can legitimately be described as 'causes' of others. But we have also seen that without prior observation and the analysis of what correlates with what, experiments may turn out to be nothing more than shots in the dark, great ideas that have only a small chance of being right because they are not grounded in the reality they are supposed to explain. Even the most dedicated experimenter can benefit from observation.

Costs of experiments are not, however, just those of time and money. There are also costs in terms of animal use, interference with animals' lives, or disruption to their environments. More and more people are becoming concerned about the welfare of animals and either want to do away with experiments on animals altogether or to at least feel that experiments only take place if they are really necessary. A key part of establishing the likely benefit of an experiment is being able to make the case that the results are likely to be important, which in turn means that they are likely to be decisive and either refute or support a critical hypothesis. The better the observations beforehand and the more a case has been built up from observing what happens in 'natural experiments', the more convincing the case for a manipulative experiment will be.

Observation that replaces or at least postpones experimental manipulation thus contributes directly to animal welfare through a potential reduction in the number of animals that might have to be used in the experiments. Not only that, but someone who has acquired a good knowledge of their animals through having watched them carefully beforehand, is likely to be able to carry out the experiments in a much more animal-friendly way, for example, through understanding the animals' needs for shelter or social companions. Observation can thus contribute both to a Reduction in the numbers of animals used as well as to a Refinement of experimental procedures. If, in addition, it leads to the Replacement of experiments altogether, it makes a major contribution to each one of what have come to be called the 'three Rs' of animal experimentation: Reduction, Refinement and Replacement (Russell and Burch, 1959) . Observation should therefore be seen as one of the major 'alternatives' to animal experimentation, a way of providing scientific data of a high standard while safeguarding animal welfare at the same time.

There is another great advantage to being an observer in the real world as opposed to someone who controls precisely and experimentally what their animals do. You don't have the problems of keeping and looking after the animals. Either the animals are looking after themselves or someone else is doing it for you. For laboratory experiments on animals, the costs of housing and caring for the animals are now often so great as to be almost prohibitive for all but the largest institutions. Fulfilling all the current regulations about standards of cages and hygiene costs a great deal of money before a study is even started. By observing animals in the wild, you have, by comparison, very little initial expenditure. You may have to travel to get to where the wild animals live, you may also choose to augment your observations with equipment that may be costly, and you should, of course, observe Health and Safety rules, but the animals are there for free. No costly housing. No need to pay for new ventilation or heating systems. No need to worry if they can take care of themselves when you aren't there.

Animals in zoos and on farms come with similar advantages, except that here they are being taken care of by other people. Farmers and zoos are already keeping animals, for commercial or other reasons, on a scale that is far greater than could be afforded by an individual even with a large research grant. Imagine trying to keep 100 giraffes in a laboratory. By observing on farms and zoos, you are therefore hugely cutting down on your research costs, with the further advantage that the results will have immediate practical application to the farms and zoos themselves.

1.8 Plan of the book

This book is arranged to help you plan and carry out your own project on animal behaviour from initial idea through planning, collecting data, analysing the results, and then writing a report on what you have observed. We start by surveying the broad sweep of animal behaviour so that you can see the range of questions that can be asked about it. We will see that asking the right question is the key to the subsequent success of any research, but that it is particularly so for an observational approach where the difficulties of collecting the data (cold, wet fieldwork, for example) means that it is essential to focus on collecting only that data that is really essential. Paradoxically, the new technologies that make it so much easier to collect vast quantities of information only make the formulation of precise questions even more important. Without a clear question, we could drown in a surfeit of data, not knowing what it is telling us. In Chapters 3 and 4, we look the principles of research design, which are strikingly the same for both observational and experimental research. Chapter 5 takes us further into the planning that has to go into any successful research project and Chapter 6 is a guide on how to collect observational data. Chapter 7 looks at the particular problems of observing on farms, in zoos, and in the wild and in Chapters 8 and 9, we turn to the analysis of different sorts data, using some real examples that have all yielded important results despite using the minimum of equipment. Finally, in Chapter 10, we look back to what we have learnt, and forward to the future in which new observational approaches are being opened up to us.

Throughout the book, there is a positive message of going both backwards and forwards. We go backwards to the roots of ethology with its emphasis on observing what animals do in their natural environments, and we go forwards with new sets of equipment and analytic tools that make observation a more powerful and quantitative approach to the study of animal behaviour than it has ever been before. Observation has always had animal welfare and naturalness on its side. Now it has technology and statistics and acknowledged standards of research design to help it too. It is a force to be reckoned with, alongside and sometimes instead of, experimentation. As we are now about to see, it is an extremely powerful way of both asking and answering questions about animal behaviour.

2 Asking the right question

Niko Tinbergen, (see Fig. 2.1) whose pioneering work on animal behaviour we touched on in the last chapter, had the ability to stop seminar speakers in their tracks by saying simply: 'And exactly what question are you asking?' Eminent people, with complex diagrams on the board, or students with boxfuls of painstakingly collected data, would suddenly realize to their horror that they had not been entirely clear in formulating a hypothesis, or that they did not know quite what sort of data would count for it or against it. They had perhaps thought that if they collected enough data, or built a complex enough model, something interesting would emerge. Niko, jabbing the air with his home-rolled cigarette, the ash dangling precariously from its end, would gently point out that perhaps the reason they hadn't found answers might be because they hadn't asked the right questions or, worse, had confused different types of question.

If this were just a historical anecdote, we could note it and pass on. The Maestro, as Niko was known, would perhaps have become a little more real to people who never knew him but remain as a mystical 'founding father' not really relevant to us today. But unfortunately, the lessons that the Maestro tried to teach us have still not been fully absorbed. The reason why his classic paper on aims and methods (1963) is still important and worth reading today is that many people are still inadvertently making the same mistakes, and are confused by just the same issues that Niko was addressing all those years ago. In particular, people still confuse questions about adaptation (how does the behaviour enhance reproductive success?) with questions about causation (what is the mechanism underlying the behaviour?), not realizing that although both are valid questions in their own right, they require quite different sets of information to answer them.

This chapter is about the different kinds of question you can ask about animal behaviour and then how you can formulate a hypothesis that is precise enough to make it clear what you need to do to answer that question. It is almost impossible to over-state the importance to the ultimate success of a project of taking time to turn a vague question into a testable hypothesis. The right question determines not only the kind of data you need to collect (for example, data collected over the whole lifetime of the animals or at just

Fig. 2.1 Niko Tinbergen was a pioneer of wildlife filming. Photograph by Lary Shaffer.

selected moments in time) but what you need to record, how often, how long for, and how many animals you need to watch to get valid results. It will determine what equipment you need, whether you can break off your observations periodically, or need to make continuous observations all day. It will determine whether you need to know your animals as individuals or can treat them as a single flock or herd. It will completely and utterly determine whether your project is a success or a failure because what you are trying to do is to collect the data that will either support or refute a particular hypothesis. It doesn't matter if your hypothesis is wrong, but it does matter whether you have collected the right data in the right way to show that it is definitely wrong. Get the question right, specify the hypothesis you are testing correctly, and then see whether the predictions of that hypothesis match up to what goes on in the real world, and you will be on the right track. Ask a confused question, be unclear about what it really means, or not know what data would count either for it or against it, and you are heading for disaster, however much work you subsequently put in.

The trick is to go from a general 'wondering' type question to one that is specific enough to be answerable with the time and resources available. You may find this vaguely disappointing. The highly specific question, focussing on one aspect of behaviour, will not answer all the questions you might possibly want to ask about your animals, but that is exactly the point. You can't find out everything there is to know all at once. You have to specialize and be content to have contributed a small brick in a larger edifice. If you are lucky, that small brick will have wider implications and contribute to an understanding of other species or of animal behaviour generally. But your job, at the moment of collecting the data, is to make sure the brick is sound.

Better a small, watertight brick that does the job required of it, than a large pile that rapidly disintegrates into rubble when examined critically, however exciting it looked at first.

We start, then, with a general view of the kinds of questions that can be asked about animal behaviour and the ways in which observation can contribute to all of them. This will prepare us for Chapters 3 and 4 where we take the next steps and move from broad, general questions to the formulation and testing of more specific hypotheses.

2.1 Adaptation: how behaviour contributes to life, sex, and reproductive success

In his *Just So Stories*, Rudyard Kipling (1902) puts forward a number of charming ideas about how animals got to be the way they are. The elephant's trunk, for example, is the result of an encounter between a baby elephant and a crocodile. No elephant, at that time, had a trunk—just a nose the size of a boot. One day, while the elephant was standing at the side of a river, the crocodile grabbed hold of its nose and tried to pull the elephant into the water. The elephant resisted and the tug-of-war that followed resulted in the elephant's nose being pulled and pulled until it was the length we see today. Thereafter, all elephants had extra long noses or trunks.

Unfortunately, many people are under the impression that when biologists suggest a hypothesis about the adaptiveness of behaviour—why starlings fly in such large groups, for example, or why gulls foot-paddle in mud—they are doing nothing more than putting forward a slightly more sophisticated type of a 'Just-So' story—vaguely plausible but completely untestable and therefore not part of real science. 'Adaptation' is seen by many as a game of pure speculation, in which anybody and everybody can join in because there is no possible evidence that would make one person's guess any more or less likely than another's. This widespread but totally erroneous view owes much to a paper by Stephen J. Gould and Richard Lewontin called *The Spandrels of San Marco and the Panglossian Paradigm* (1979) in which the term 'Adaptationist' (someone who believes in the power of natural selection) was used in almost derogatory way, to imply a naïve and unquestioning view of evolution. Many of the points that Gould and Lewontin make in this paper are very important, for example, that animals may not always be perfectly adapted and that some traits, such as the redness of blood, may not be adaptations in their own right at all but by-products of selection for something else, in this case, oxygen-carrying ability. But the straw man they set up to attack—the biologist who believes that all animals are perfectly adapted to every aspect of their environment—is just that, a straw man. Richard Dawkins (1982) lists many of the ways in which natural selection often fails to achieve perfect adaptation in *The Extended Phenotype* (Chapter 3) and no-one would accuse him of underestimating the power of natural selection!

2.2   Adaptive hypotheses can be tested

What Gould and Lewontin (1979) seemed to be unaware of, or chose to ignore, however, was that adaptive hypotheses can be tested just like any other scientific hypothesis. Such hypotheses make predictions that either do or do not match what happens in the real world, and they are then either accepted or discarded accordingly. If you do decide to test an adaptive hypothesis, therefore, it is just as essential to understand what would count as evidence against your hypothesis as it is to know what would count as evidence in its favour. You have to set up a situation where, if your adaptive explanation is true, you would get one set of results and if it were false, something else would happen. Some people, too readily following Gould and Lewontin, are under the impression that adaptive hypotheses cannot be refuted, because they do not understand what evidence would lead to an adaptive hypothesis being discarded. They believe that whatever the evidence, adaptive hypotheses always stand. Someone just moves the goal posts.

This belief is so widespread but so mistaken that we need to deal with it before we can understand how adaptive hypotheses can be tested in practice. To call something an 'adaptation' implies that there is some feature—a behaviour pattern, a wing shape, a particularly robust immune system—that allows the animal possessing it to escape death or reproductive failure in a way that animals without that adaptation cannot. All supposed adaptations are therefore implied comparisons between animals that do and animals that do not possess the feature in question. But where are the unsuccessful animals without that feature that we need to make such a comparison? If our adaptive hypothesis is correct, they should either have died out long ago or be instantly eliminated if they arise by mutation in the present day. Either way, they should not be around to show us what losers they are.

Now we can see why testing adaptive hypotheses is sometimes thought be so difficult as to be effectively impossible. It appears to involve a comparison between living animals and hypothetical failures that do not exist. This is not, however, an accurate description of the situation at all. Within one species, there will be living animals that show variation in behaviour and appearance and so can be compared to each other. Some males will have longer or more ornamented tails than others. Some individual animals will be bolder than others when predators are around. Natural selection will have eliminated animals that show extreme behaviour (such as males with tails so long they cannot fly, or animals that are so fearless that they fall inevitably victim to predators) but there will often be some that hide for longer or shorter periods than average or are more or less cautious when they do come out into the open. We can make use of this variation to test adaptive hypotheses by seeing what happens to animals that, say, spend different amounts of time looking for food and hiding from predators.

This naturally occurring variation could, of course, be increased by experimentally manipulating living animals, for example, by cutting or lengthening their tails feathers or painting them different colours, an approach that is discussed more fully elsewhere (Dawkins, 1995). However, as this is a book about observation with an emphasis on minimal interference with the animals themselves, we will concentrate here on some powerful observational methods for testing adaptive hypotheses without such manipulation. Observation is particularly important for studies of adaptation because we are asking questions about how natural selection has shaped the behaviour of undisturbed animals in the wild.

There are three ways in which adaptive hypotheses can be tested with observations:

(i) Observations of different individuals within a single species;
(ii) Observations of individuals from different species;
(iii) Observations of animals in comparison to man-made machines or computer models.

2.2.1 Comparing individuals within a species

One of the most spectacular examples of testing an adaptive hypothesis through observation comes from a study of the behaviour of Thomson's gazelles (*Gazella thomsoni*) in the Serengeti National Park in Tanzania (Fitzgibbon and Fanshawe, 1988). It was spectacular because it involved following wild dogs (*Lycaon pictus*) as they chased groups of gazelles and recording which individuals the dogs caught and killed. Thomson's gazelles, in common with other gazelle species, show a very curious behaviour known as 'stotting',—where an animal in full flight from a predator will suddenly spring into the air with all four feet off the ground, giving the appearance of bouncing up and down as it runs. The behaviour is puzzling because it is not clear how jumping up and down can be adaptive when danger is so close and when it would seem that running directly away from the predator as fast as possible would be at a premium. At least eleven different adaptive hypotheses have been suggested to explain why gazelles stott. These include the proposal that it might give the stotting gazelle a better view of the predator or that it might be a warning signal to the other members of the herd, a bit like an alarm call.

Fitzgibbon and Fanshawe, however, tested an alternative hypothesis: that stotting is a signal to the predators about the physical condition of the stotter and specifically that it indicates that it has the stamina to keep going on a long chase. Some individual gazelles are capable of outrunning wild dogs and hyenas if they keep running for long enough and fast enough, so it would clearly be in the predators' interests not to waste their time and effort chasing gazelles they are not going to be able to catch. The 'pursuit deterrence' hypothesis sees stotting as an indicator to the predator that the stotter is not worth chasing—effectively a signal to the predator that says: 'don't even think about chasing me as I shall out-run you in the end'.

The pursuit deterrence hypothesis makes a number of predictions, all of which are testable by further observation. It is thus not in the category of *Just So* stories at all, but open to being refuted if its predictions turn out to be wrong. For example, one of its predictions is that wild dogs should be less likely to chase gazelles that are stotting vigorously (many jumps/minute) than gazelles that are doing it only half-heartedly or not at all (fewer or no stotts/minute). Another is that stotters should be in better physical condition, be better runners, and less likely to be caught if they are chased, than non-stotters. A third prediction is that if stotting is a signal to predators before they have decided which individual to chase, most stotting should occur right at the beginning of a chase and when the predators are close. Each of these predictions was tested by observation, making use of the fact that different individual gazelles naturally stotted at different rates. Was a gazelle's fate apparent from its stotting rate?

Fitzgibbon and Fanshawe followed herds of gazelles when they were approached by wild dogs. They found that stotting only occurred if the dogs actually started chasing. Then, as the hunt got under way, the dogs would concentrate their attention on a few individual gazelles and selectively chase them. The researchers recorded the stotting rate (stotts/minute) of a gazelle the dogs had chosen to chase and compared this with that of a 'control' gazelle—the nearest adult gazelle that was also running away but had not been singled out by the dogs. The control animals were apparently equally vulnerable and available but they were not being chased. Nevertheless, the gazelles singled out by the dogs stotted significantly less than the control animals running alongside them. This result supported the first prediction of the pursuit deterrence hypothesis, that dogs would pick out the less vigorous stotters as victims, but it also illustrates how careful we have to be in concluding that the dogs were chasing some gazelles *because* they stotted less.

The negative correlation between stotting rate and chances of being chased is evidence in favour of the pursuit deterrence hypothesis, but, as we saw in Chapter 1, correlation does not necessarily mean causation. It could be, for example, that dogs did not choose low rate stotters but that, once a gazelle realized it was being chased, it lowered its stotting rate and concentrated on running. It is not clear which direction the causal arrow is pointing: is less vigorous stotting the cause of not being chased or does being chased cause a reduction in stotting? Fortunately, there is further evidence on this point. Some gazelles were observed both before and after they were singled out and chased by the dogs. There was no evidence that they lowered their stotting rate as a result of being chased, which would suggest that the dogs were genuinely avoiding the higher rate stotters.

The second prediction of the pursuit deterrence hypothesis was also borne out by observing the fates of different gazelles. If a gazelle was chased, it was less likely to be caught if it was a vigorous stotter (that is, it stotted more than the control animal running alongside it). Higher rate stotters did indeed appear to be better at running and escaping. Furthermore, during the dry season, when the body condition of all gazelles was low, stotting also became less common. Stotting could thus be said to be an 'honest' indicator of body condition and stamina in the sense that animals in poor body condition simply could not stott vigorously. Wild dogs, being the canny hunters they are, learn to recognize the tell tale signs of what is and what isn't worth chasing.

Observation also supported the third prediction of the hypothesis: stotting was most likely to occur at the very beginning of a hunt when the wild dogs were very close. For the dogs, this was the time when they were least likely to have chosen their victim and when, for a gazelle, it was most important to signal its superior running ability. The gazelles even altered their behaviour depending on which kind of predator was chasing them. They stotted much more to wild dogs and hyenas, which chase over long distances, and only rarely to cheetahs. The significance of this difference is that cheetahs stalk their prey, spend time watching them from quite close, and then single out their victim before they start on a short sharp chase. On a pursuit deterrence hypothesis, there would be no point stotting to a predator that had already picked its victim for a short chase, but every point in trying to deflect the interest of predators such as wild dogs that still have to make their decision before a long chase begins.

It is only rarely that we are able to see death and injury taking place in front of our eyes in quite such a dramatic way as this. More often, we have to use more indirect ways of showing that a behaviour is adaptive, but here, too, individual variation in behaviour can show us how natural selection acts in practice. Female sea turtles, for example, come ashore to lay their eggs (Fig. 2.2). They haul themselves up on the beach and dig a nest in the sand with their hind feet. Having laid their eggs and covered them with sand, they head off back to the ocean. The baby turtles, when they hatch, are on their own and have a perilous time emerging from the sand and finding their own way to the sea. Many perish before they get there, either because the sea drowns them in

Fig. 2.2   Female Hawksbill turtle laying her eggs. Photograph by Nicholas Mrosovsky.

their nests before they hatch, or because they are eaten by predators waiting for them on the beach, or just because they become disorientated and fail to find the sea at all. Clearly, exactly where a female chooses to make her nest could have a major effect on hatchling survival. Kamel and Mrosovsky (2005) showed that female Hawksbill turtles (*Eretmochelys imbricata*) in Guadeloupe differed in where they chose to lay their eggs, but that individual females were very consistent in their choice of nest site. Within the nesting season, females would come ashore every 10–20 days and lay another clutch. A given female would repeatedly choose a similar site—some consistently favouring forest areas in the upper part of the beach, some choosing the middle beach, and others always laying nearer the sea. By relating the position of nests to the numbers and size of the baby turtles that hatched from them, Kamel and Mrosovsky could test the adaptive significance of nest site selection in their mothers. Interestingly, it turned out that there was no 'best' sort of nest site, since the numbers of baby turtles successfully hatching from nests in all areas was the same, but the causes of hatchling death were different. Nests near the sea made it easy for the hatchlings to quickly gain the safety of the ocean but were subject to flooding if there was a hurricane. Nests further away from the sea stayed drier, but presented the newly hatched turtles with a more hazardous journey to the water because of predation by land crabs (*Gecarcinus lateralis*) that grabbed the baby turtles and dragged them into their burrows. Death comes in many forms and there are many different ways of avoiding it.

The turtle hatchlings that do not make it to the sea, and the gazelles hunted down by the wild dogs, both allow us to study natural selection in the raw and to test adaptive hypotheses about why the survivors survive and the others perish. However, these two examples also illustrate two quite different reasons why individuals within a species may differ in their behaviour. In the case of the gazelles, stotting seems to be an advantage in deflecting predators, but not all animals are strong enough to be able to do it at a high rate: they stott if they can, but not all of them are physically strong enough to be able to do so. With the turtles, on the other hand, it appears that there is no one perfect solution. Sometimes some nest sites are best and in other years, different ones are, so variation here is maintained not by every individual attempting to do the same thing and only some being able to, but by there being a positive advantage to doing things differently.

In many cases, however, there are logistical problems in actually witnessing death and destruction as directly as in these two examples. You could watch a flock of birds for days on end and never once see a cat catch any of them, even though we know that cats account for a large number of bird kills. Fortunately, we don't always have to wait until we see animals actually die before we can test adaptive hypotheses. We can look for tell-tale differences in behaviour.

For example, in testing adaptive hypotheses about why a particular species adopts a very social way of life and goes round in groups (Krause and Ruxton, 2002), you may not be able to witness the deaths of solitary members of the same species or determine exactly what happens to the animals that leave a group, but you may well be able to make observations to show that solitary animals or those on the very edge of the group behave differently in ways that affect their survival. They may be more wary, spend more time looking around, or spend less time feeding than those at the centre. You might not see any solitary animals actually die of starvation, but you might well observe that they consistently get less to eat. You would then have uncovered a potentially serious disadvantage of not being in a group, enough to infer that one of the benefits of group living was related to getting more to eat. Or, you might show that animals on their own respond less quickly to the appearance of a predator than those in a large group. This would suggest an anti-predator advantage to group living, despite your not actually seeing any deaths from predation. In other words, even in a relatively short project, too short to measure survival or reproductive success itself, you can collect enough observational evidence to show that solitary animals are more at risk and go some way to showing what those risks are.

As we have stressed all along, of course, it is important to be aware of the limitations of such correlations. Perhaps the ones on their own are younger, or less experienced, or diseased in some way, and that is the real reason why they appear to be more at risk than the groupies. Perhaps the larger groups have chosen an area where there is a particularly rich source of food and that is why they feed more and look up less (Elgar 1989).

While it is important to be aware of such possibilities, however, it is also important not to be deterred by them. In fact, the best way of dealing with them is usually to collect even more (observational) data. For example, Emlen and Wrege (1989) were investigating the adaptive significance of helpers at the nest in white-fronted bee-eaters (*Merops bullockoides*), and ran into exactly this kind of problem. Bee-eaters are brightly coloured, colonially nesting birds that make their nests by tunnelling into the walls of earthy cliffs. Like the jackals we met in the last chapter (section 1.5), juveniles often stay and help their parents for two to three years and, like the jackals, older parents would tend to have more helpers than younger parents. Just as in the jackal study, there was thus a potential difficulty in separating out the effect of how much help the helpers were actually giving from all the other possible contributors to parental nesting success, such as age and experience. What Emlen and Wrege did was to measure as many of these other factors as they could and so they were able to control for them when they did their analysis. They knew the age of the parents that did and did not have helpers and they knew how much breeding experience they had too. They knew the age of the juveniles that stayed to help and that of the ones that set up their own territories and reared broods of their own. Then, when they came to do their comparison between parents with different numbers of helpers and parents with no helpers at all, they knew they were comparing like with like. They compared parents of the same age and nesting experience and were able to show statistically that they still had more surviving offspring the more helpers they had. This statistical approach indicated a causal connection between helpers and chick survival because the correlation could not be explained by other factors, at least not the factors that had been specifically measured and controlled for. The small lingering doubt that there might have been some factors they had not thought of was more than compensated for by the fact that they drew their conclusions from the behaviour of animals in their natural environment and with minimal interference to the animals themselves.

2.2.2 Comparing species

Observing the fates of different individuals of the same species is not, however, the only way we have of testing adaptive hypotheses. Another very powerful approach is to look at the range of species alive today and analyse the reasons both for their success and their diversity. The very fact that species are different—that lions are not tigers, for example—shows that it is possible to be successful in different ways. We can use these differences to see what it takes to be successful in different environments and test different adaptive hypotheses against what different animals actually do.

An observational study by Esther Cullen (1957) showed how this can work. Cullen compared the behaviour of two closely related species of gulls that nest in very different environments: black-headed gulls and kittiwakes. Black-headed gulls (*Larus ridibundus*) nest on the ground, live in large noisy colonies, and mount group attacks on predators such as foxes and crows by dive-bombing and mobbing them. Their close relatives, the kittiwakes (*Rissa tridactyla*), by contrast, nest high up on tiny cliff ledges where neither ground predators nor aerial predators such as large gulls and crows can reach them. Kittiwakes are thus essentially free from the predation that is such a constant threat throughout the nesting season for black-headed gulls. By comparing the behaviour of the two species, Cullen was able to demonstrate that many features of black-headed gull behaviour can be seen as adaptations to this constant threat of predation. Black-headed gulls pick up and remove empty egg shells as soon as each chick is dry, whereas kittiwakes never do this. As a result, black-headed gull nests are clean and inconspicuous, whereas kittiwakes have messy, conspicuous nests, full of guano and old bits of shell (Fig. 2.3). This difference supports the hypothesis (Tinbergen, 1959) that the behaviour of removing egg-shells is an anti-predator adaptation in black-headed gulls.

Further confirmation of this comes from observations on other ground-nesting bird species, which also show the same behaviour, even though they

Fig. 2.3   Nesting kittiwakes. Perched on tiny cliff ledges, the nests are safe from both ground and flying predators. Photograph by Niko Tinbergen.

may be only distantly related to black-headed gulls. The bittern (*Botaurus stellaris*), a relative of the herons, is also a ground nester with a camouflaged nest and also carefully removes empty egg shells from its nest once the chicks have hatched. In this respect, black-headed gulls and bitterns behave more like each other than the black-headed gull does to its much closer relative, the kittiwake. Black-headed gulls and bitterns show *convergent* evolution—independent evolution of a trait in response to a common threat, in this case predation on a nest on the ground.

Convergent evolution provides good evidence for adaptation because it shows how unrelated species can evolve similar behaviour when subjected to the same selection pressures. But to make this approach really convincing, it is necessary to look at more than just two or three species. Since Cullen's study, the technique of testing adaptive hypotheses by looking for convergent evolution has been developed into a major mathematical tool so that it is now possible to compare large numbers of different species (Grafen 1989; Harvey and Pagel, 1991). The Comparative Method, as it is known, looks for correlations between features of behaviour or morphology on the one hand and ecological factors on the other. If the same habit or structure evolves independently in different groups of animals whenever they live in certain habitats, then that is good evidence that the convergent trait is an adaptation to similar ecological factors.

One striking use of the Comparative Method is to test adaptive hypotheses about why testes are the size they are. Males of some species have small testes and make relatively small amounts of sperm whereas males of other species, often closely related to them, have large testes and make much larger amounts of sperm. A male gorilla (*Gorilla gorilla*) weighs more than four times as much as a male chimpanzee (*Pan troglodytes*) but has testes that are less than one quarter of the weight of a chimpanzee's. Short (1979) proposed that testis size is adapted to the amount of competition a male faces from the sperm of other males. In species where females mate with only one male, that male will be able to ensure paternity with no competition. But in species where females mate with many males, the sperm from those different males will compete to fertilize her eggs. Those males that produce the largest quantities of sperm and therefore have the largest testes are likely to be the most successful: large testes are thus seen as an adaptation to out-compete the sperm of other males. This would certainly explain the difference between gorillas and chimpanzees because gorilla males, although they mate with many females, have a monopoly over them, whereas chimpanzees have a highly promiscuous mating system. Chimpanzee sperm therefore has to face much more competition from other males than does gorilla sperm.

The sperm competition hypothesis can be tested more rigorously by comparing a much wider range of primate species than just these two and seeing whether the correlation between testis size and mating habits still holds. In fact, it does (Harcourt et al., 1981). The species that live in multi-male groups, where sperm competition is intense, have much larger testes than those that live either as monogamous pairs or with a 'harem' system of one male and many females, as is found in gorillas. This latter point is particularly interesting because it allows us to distinguish between two different adaptive explanations of large testis size. Since males that mate with many females but without competition from other males have testes that are similar in size to those of monogamous males, this shows that it is not the number of females a male mates with that affects testis size. It is whether or not those females are likely to have sex with other males. This is exactly what would be expected if testis size were adapted to degree of sperm competition. It is not what would be expected on the alternative, and perhaps more obvious, adaptive hypothesis that testis size is adapted to the number of females a male mates with. The sperm competition hypothesis also explains the distribution of testis size in other species of mammals, as well as birds and fish, where there is a similar relationship between testis size, sperm production, and mating patterns (Harvey and Pagel, 1991). The fact that males from completely different species adopt a common solution to a common problem is good evidence for the theory that large testes are an adaptation to ensure paternity in the face of female promiscuity.

Testing adaptive hypotheses using the Comparative Method is entirely feasible for a short term research project, although you will probably do best to find someone able to guide you through the complexities of the method, which are considerably greater than we have time to discuss here. You will probably not be able to collect all the necessary information yourself, simply through not having the time to observe more than one or two species. You will have to rely on other peoples' studies that are already published and scour the literature looking for studies on different species. Most of these studies will be observational—field studies of what animal actually do in the wild. The Comparative Method feeds on observation (usually other peoples' observations) with a voracious appetite. Without armies of people having done the observations in the first place, it would wither and die. The contribution that the Comparative Method has made is that it takes observations that by themselves would be interesting but of only limited importance and turns them, with a detailed analysis of a whole range of other species, into a quantitatively robust hypothesis-testing tool. But the original observations form its bedrock.

2.2.3 Comparisons with models or machines

So far, we have seen at least two ways in which we can put adaptive hypothesis to the test, either of which we could use to test the hypothesis that the reason 'why' gulls foot-paddle is that it enables them to find food buried in mud. By comparing the behaviour of different individual gulls within one species in the same environment, we could test the prediction that the foot-paddlers feed more often or are more successful at finding food. Alternatively, by comparing different species, we could use the Comparative Method and test the prediction that foot-paddling would occur most in those species which fed on prey hidden in susceptible substrates and which had suitable feet.

It may have occurred to you, however, that there is another and a more direct way of testing adaptive hypotheses about the function or results of what animals do. This is to simulate or model the behaviour. For example, to test the hypothesis that foot-paddling has an effect on mud that brings objects to the surface, you could make some little paddles roughly the size of gulls' feet and simulate the behaviour yourself on some real mud. You could look at the physical effect you were having on the mud and whether you turned up more items hidden in it. You might even be able to build a little machine that allowed you to vary the frequency with which the paddles moved to see whether the frequency with which real gull feet moved had a different effect from other kinds of movement. You would be using a modelling approach to tell you not just what affect the paddling movements were having, but even whether the frequency of those movements was the best way to detect food in mud. Your test of the hypothesis would then need further observations on real gulls to see if they foot-paddled at the predicted frequency. If you showed that they moved their feet at precisely the frequency that your model had already shown was the one to have the maximum effect on mud, you would have found a nice piece of evidence for the adaptive significance of foot-paddling.

Vogel et al. (1973) used exactly this approach to uncover the adaptive significance of the shape of prairie dog burrows. Prairie dogs (*Cynomys ludovicianus*) are large rodents that live in communal burrows. They can occur in such large numbers that they are collectively referred to as 'prairie dog towns'. A potential problem with living in burrows is getting enough ventilation through to the more distant parts. With several prairie dogs huddled together in one burrow, suffocation could become a serious issue and so a regular supply of fresh air is essential. Somehow the air has got to be made to flow in the burrows. Vogel et al. noticed that the entrances to the prairie dog burrows were built in a rather curious way. At one end, the entrance was surrounded by a steep-sided crater mound sticking a few centimetres above the ground (Fig. 2.4). At the other end, the entrance was surrounded by a low dome. Why should all the burrows have mounds at each end and why should the mounds be of different shapes?

Vogel et al. tested the hypothesis that mounds of different shapes at each end of a burrow generated air flow and were therefore an adaptation to

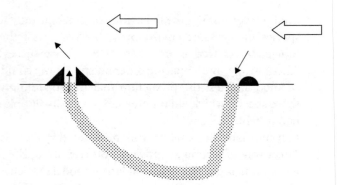

Fig. 2.4 Diagrammatic representation of a prairie dog burrow (not to scale) to illustrate how air can be drawn into it by even the slightest breeze on the surface. The higher crater mound on the left acts as a chimney. Air is drawn out of it by the surface wind and consequently fresh air is drawn into the other end of the burrow through the dome mound.

ventilating a long burrow. Their hypothesis was that small breezes on the surface would draw air out of the higher mound at one end and this would cause fresh air to be sucked into the lower mound at the other end. They tested this by building their own model tunnel and putting mounds of different shapes and sizes on each end. They then created a small wind of the same magnitude that was common on the prairies where the rodents live, and found that they could increase the air flow in their model burrow by making the mound at one end of a tunnel considerably higher than the other. Air was then continuously drawn into the burrow. They then went back and observed the real animals in more detail. They found that the prairie dog solution of having a burrow with a steep-sided crater mound at one end and a lower dome at the other, was so effective that there was a complete air change in the burrow every ten minutes, even with only a very light breeze on the surface.

Note that this demonstration of the adaptive significance of burrow shape was not tested by showing that prairie dogs with misshapen mounds on the ends of their burrows died of suffocation (the first method we discussed), nor by comparing different species living in different conditions (the second method), but was inferred from the similarity of what the animals built and what a human engineer, faced with a similar problem (how to ventilate a long tunnel), would do. The test of the hypothesis was the similarity between the two solutions, not just some vague similarity, but detailed, quantitative similarity reflected in the precise shape and size of the mounds. Alternative adaptive hypotheses, such as that the mounds are look-out points or a defence against flooding, are less convincing because they cannot account for these details. There is no reason for two look-out points at the end of one burrow to be different, or for there to be two distinct ways of stopping water going down a burrow. After they had built their model with its miniature tunnels, Vogel et al. went out into a prairie dog town and blew smoke down empty tunnels, just to see whether air in real burrows really did move as they expected. Sure enough, the smoke moved reliably through the burrows even with very little wind and whatever the wind direction. The prairie dogs had built all of the mounds symmetrically so that their ventilation system worked with every little breeze around.

Physical models of what animals do can be thought of as formalized, quantitative hypotheses that can then be put to the test to see if they apply to real animals. Vague, verbal hypotheses such as 'air might get sucked through a tunnel', or 'vibrating mud brings objects to the surface', are some help, but you could sit and speculate on the way the world might be for a very long time without really producing much evidence. But if you can formulate a more precise mathematical model or build an actual physical model that accomplishes what a living animal does, you have a very much more plausible and complete hypothesis to test. You know it could work, whereas a vague verbal hypothesis might be full of contradictions or inconsistencies that you were not aware of. Your machine or physical model might not do things in exactly the same as an animal does, but your model will generate some quantitative and testable predictions—such as the precise size and shape of mounds, or the precise frequency of vibration of feet—so that you will be able to see how closely it matches the behaviour of real animals. You know the model is not breaking the laws of physics and you know what to do to test it.

Sometimes it is not even necessary to build a real physical model. A virtual or computer model can be a powerful way of hypothesis generation and testing too. Because computer models have to be expressed more mathematically and precisely than verbal ones, they too can show up inconsistencies in less precisely expressed ideas and come up with some surprising and testable predictions of their own. Just as a real model has to mimic the actual physical movements or results of how an animal behaves, a virtual model stands or falls by whether its quantitative predictions describe the behaviour of real animals. For example, several different adaptive hypotheses have been put forward to explain why many fish swim in groups or shoals, including the possibility that it gives them protection by confusing any predator that attacks them, or that they can save energy by swimming together, rather in the way that cyclists sometimes make use of the 'slip stream' of trucks or of each other in cycle races. The energy saving hypothesis can be modelled mathematically, using information from hydrodynamics to show how fish could swim to save energy. Weihs (1975) realized that shoaling fish could potentially save energy in two ways: by pushing water against the fish swimming alongside them and by using the vortices produced by fish swimming in front of them. The energy saving hypothesis makes very clear predictions about how fish should position themselves to gain the most advantage in both these ways depending on their size, shape, and swimming speed. The hypothesis predicts that fish within a shoal should swim a certain distance from their nearest neighbours on each side to gain maximum energy from pushing, and they should remain a certain distance from the fish in front to gain maximum energy from the vortices they leave behind (Fig. 2.5). If the hypothesis really could predict precise shoaling patterns in fish, this would be powerful evidence that the shoaling itself was an adaptation to save energy. In practice, it can't (Weihs, 1975). Its predictions about how fish position themselves while swimming are not upheld, at least in saithe, herring, and cod. These fish swim further away from their lateral neighbours and closer to the fish in front than the energy saving hypothesis predicts they

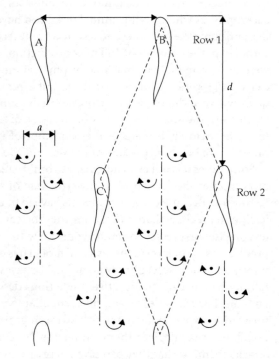

Fig. 2.5   Fish can save energy from the swimming of other fish in two ways. Firstly, fish C, midway between A and B, receives induced velocity from the spinning vortices shed by A and B. As the vortices do not stabilize immediately, fish C should stay at least five tail-beats behind them. Secondly, fish swimming close together (e.g. A and B) can push off one another. Maximum energy saving occurs of the fish are 0.3 body lengths apart. In three species of fish (saithe, herring, and cod) fish kept two or three times too far away from lateral neighbours and swam too close to fish in front to gain maximum energy saving. From Weihs, 1975. Permission not yet obtained.

should. Energy saving might be a small benefit to fish but it does not seem, at least in these species, to be the main adaptive explanation for why they swim together. Here is a clear case of an adaptive hypothesis being tested and, in this case rejected, because observations on real animals did not fit its predictions.

Far from being untestable then, as claimed by Gould and Lewontin, adaptive questions readily yield to different kinds of observational test. Different adaptive hypotheses make different predictions and they are just as vulnerable to disproof as any other kind of hypothesis. They are most vulnerable (and therefore most convincing if they do hold up), when the predictions are surprising, quantitative, and distinct from those of other adaptive hypotheses, a theme we will return to in Chapter 3. Because adaptive questions are often best answered by looking at the undisturbed behaviour of animals in the environment in which they evolved, observation has a dominant position in the study of adaptation; guiding, supplementing, and sometimes replacing experimentation altogether.

We have also seen that the most serious objection to an observational approach—that it cannot distinguish causation from correlation—can be answered to a very large extent by measuring many variables at a time and adopting a statistical approach (section 2.2.2). There are still 'controls' but the controls are those of how observations are taken. A running gazelle is compared with a 'control' gazelle running alongside it. Parents with helpers are compared with control parents that have no helpers. The Comparative Method similarly uses a statistical approach to compare different species and to find those ecological factors that best fit the data. Modelling, either in the form of computer simulation or real physical models that mimic what real animals are doing, allow us to do experiments but at one remove from the animals themselves. With any of these three methods, adaptive hypotheses may stand or they may fall, exactly as any other scientific hypothesis has to do, but the gulls, paddling away in the harbour, are left in peace.

2.3   Causation: mechanisms of behaviour

Questions about adaptation are not, however, the only ones we can ask through observation. We can also ask another type of question—about what causes behaviour to occur. Causal questions are ones that try to uncover the mechanisms underlying behaviour, such as what stimulates gulls to start foot-paddling, how they manage to perform the actions, how they respond to the sight of other gulls doing it, and so on. Causal questions are about how an animal's brain, hormones, muscles, and every other part of its body contribute to its actions, and so ultimately take us from behaviour into physiology.

Causal and adaptive questions are related but distinct. Why foot-paddling is favoured by natural selection is the adaptive question. How the gull's body is built so that it does the behaviour in the right way, in the right place, and at the right time, are causal questions. The distinction between them can be further illustrated by going back to another example we have already discussed. When baby turtles hatch on a beach, they have to find their way to the sea. Many of them are killed by predators before they reach the relative safety of the ocean and so the adaptive significance of finding their way to the sea as fast as possible is clear: if they don't find it, they will die. But *how* do they find it? Is it the smell, sound, sight of the sea, or some other cue? What is the immediate stimulus that causes them to move towards it? These are the causal questions. It turns out that vision is particularly important (Salmon et al., 1992). Hatchlings are attracted to a bright shiny light which the moon-lit sea often presents.

You might be tempted to think that causal questions—about the mechanisms controlling behaviour—are good examples of questions that can be answered only by experiment, and laboratory experiment at that. After all, if we want to find out which cue an animal is using to recognize something, like egg-shells or the sea, the obvious way to investigate this is to experimentally manipulate the cues available to it and see which ones turn the behaviour on or off. As with adaptive questions, however, the answer is both yes and no. Yes, experimental manipulation is the ultimate test that the right causal factors have been identified but no, there is still also a major role for observation before, and sometimes even instead of, doing experiments. Even with causal questions, observation can sometimes go where experimental manipulation simply cannot venture.

Dorothy Cheney and Robert Seyfarth, whose work on monkey alarm calls we discussed in the last chapter (section 1.4) also used an observational approach to show something even more remarkable: that vervet monkeys know who the kin and associates of other monkeys are. They don't just know the other monkeys in their group as individuals. They know about that individual's social circle as well.

These results did not come from experiments. They came from many hours of watching and recording vervet behaviour, particularly aggressive behaviour—fighting, tail-pulling, threats, and so on. Cheney and Seyfarth observed that if a monkey had a fight with another individual, the next time those two monkeys met it was quite clear that they both remembered what had happened, because subsequent relations between them were also likely to be more aggressive. A fight made another fight more likely. But a fight between two monkeys also made a fight between the associates (friends and relatives) of those two monkeys more likely, even though those other monkeys were not themselves involved in the original fight. The members of one gang take it upon themselves to be aggressive to members of another gang just because of their social relationship with the ones who did the fighting.

This evidence that vervet monkeys have such a highly developed sense of social relationships comes entirely from observation—recording who fought whom, who sat next to whom, and who groomed whom—and then extracting a pattern from these observations, techniques we will discuss further in Chapter 9. Observation revealed who the friends of each monkey were. Observation revealed who fought with whom and what happened subsequently. Quantitative information about frequencies of behavioural interactions revealed a non-obvious but very real cause of aggression—the monkeys' knowledge of what has happened in the past between other members of their group.

Observation again played a central role in a now classic paper on animal communication. Tim Clutton-Brock and Steve Albon (1979) watched encounters between Red Deer stags (*Cervus elaphus*) on the isle of Rhum, which is just off the west coast of Scotland. During the mating season, the stags challenge each other for possession of groups of females and do so with deep guttural roars (see Fig. 2.6). By observing a large number of such encounters between stags of different sizes, Clutton-Brock and Albon noticed that not all of the challenges lead to fighting. Sometimes the stags would simply roar at each other and, after a while, the challenger would simply give up and go away. Usually, however, he did not go away immediately, but engaged in what appeared to be a roaring contest. The contest would begin

Fig. 2.6   Roaring Red Deer stag. © Roger whiteway/istockphoto.

in a relatively low key way. One stag would roar a few times and then the other would answer by roaring at a slightly higher rate. Then the first one would 'up the anti' and give more roars, and the roaring match would escalate until both stags were roaring ferociously. Then one of two things could happen. Either one of the stags would just give up, apparently outroared, or the encounter would proceed to the next stage, which consisted of the two stags pacing up and down in parallel. What caused a stag to either give up or keep going? Clutton Brock and Albon concluded that the stags were using their opponent's maximum rate of roaring relative to their own. Roaring at a high rate is a difficult thing to do because each individual roar is loud and demands considerable effort. Delivering many roars at high rate is very exhausting, and so being able to roar at a high rate is a good indicator of a stag's likely ability to sustain a major fight. Only stags that can roar well can fight well, so Clutton-Brock and Albon proposed that a roaring match is a good indicator of what would happen in a real fight, only safer. In support of this hypothesis, they observed that big stags in good condition could, when provoked, roar at the highest rate and, more importantly, that actual fights developed only between stags that were very closely matched in body size and condition. The roaring matches sorted out the men from the boys, the subsequent walking up and down gave each stag a chance to inspect the other one in more detail, and only if there was no clear indication of who would win the fight did the real aggression ensue. The cause of one stag giving up was thus being outroared by another stag. The remarkable thing was that the challenger was able to use the comparison between his own maximum roaring rate and the roaring rate of the other stag as the cue to whether to escalate or retreat. The correlations that the researchers had observed between roaring rate, relative body size, and fighting, also seemed to be the stimulus being used by the stags themselves.

Vervet monkeys and stags are just two examples of the many ways in which causal questions about animal behaviour have been answered by observational studies. Experiments were sometimes done in addition to the observations or to confirm a hypothesis, but in many cases where the observations are good enough, they are the icing on the cake, the confirmation of what was known anyway from observation. For example, Clutton-Brock and Albon showed experimentally that roaring rate was an important cue to the stags by hiding a tape recorder behind a wall and then playing roars at different rates. The fact that the stags did respond to this experimental manipulation, and even gave up on hearing the tape recorder roaring at a 'super stag' rate, is of course important confirmation of their ideas; but showing that stags respond to tape-recorded roars without the prior observations of how roars are used in context would have been much less convincing. It was the observations and the correlations between behaviour, body size, and fight outcome that had been established beforehand that originally revealed the causal basis of what triggers different stages and outcomes in a fight.

2.4   Development of behaviour

Questions about the development of behaviour concern how behaviour gets to be the way it is in the individual, such as what animals learn from their parents or how they develop a particular skill. Such questions are particularly suited to observational studies because many of the interesting questions about development only arise when there is already a good observational basis for what needs to be explained in the first place. Observations that chimpanzees use stone tools to crack open nuts, for example, led to people asking a whole range of questions about how much they understood about what sort of stones were best, and whether they taught their young the nut-cracking techniques (Boesch, 1991). Without detailed observations of how chimpanzees actually do crack open nuts, these questions would not even have been raised.

Allen and Clarke (2005) showed how it is possible to study the importance of a mother's behaviour on the development of food preferences in white-tailed ptarmigan chicks in a completely natural setting—the Rocky Mountains of California (Fig. 2.7). Ptarmigan (*Lagopus leucurus*) hens have a special call that they give when they have found food plants. The chicks respond by rushing to the indicated plant and feeding. The female vocalizes and pecks at the food, which stimulates the chicks to join her in feeding from the selected plant. Allen and Clarke wanted to know whether the chicks were actually learning what food plants to eat from their mothers. By quietly sitting close to wild ptarmigan with chicks, they were able to see what plants the hens were eating themselves and which food plants they both ate and gave the food calls to. They found that there was a clear correlation between the food plants where the mother gave the food call and the food plants in the chick's diet. Female ptarmigan were most likely to give the food call to high protein plants and, as a result, the chicks selectively ate these high protein foods out of all the ones available to them in the environment. High protein plants are critical for their growth. The mother ptarmigan was thus influencing the diet of her chicks through her own food preferences and her vocalizations.

In a completely different context, observational studies maybe the main source of information available in the study of behaviour in zoo animals, where any experimental manipulation maybe considered unethical or be logistically impossible. Many zoos have only a few animals of each species, and it may be very difficult to get a picture of 'typical' members of that species just from one zoo, or to do anything that resembles a proper experiment. However, by combining observations from animals kept in different zoos, and

Fig. 2.7   Jennifer Clarke and ptarmigan. Photograph by Stephen P. Mackessy.

making use of the fact that there will inevitably be differences between zoos in how they have reared their animals, it is often possible to put together a composite picture of the effect of different factors on the subsequent development of behaviour (Chapter 7).

For reasons completely beyond their control, zoos often have groups of animals that have been put together just because they are the same species. Martin (2005) studied groups of chimpanzees where the individuals had very different social experiences, such as being reared by their own mothers in a social group, reared without their mothers but in a group of other chimpanzees, or reared by humans without other chimpanzees. By studying 43 chimpanzees with these different social experiences from 5 zoos across the UK, he tested the hypothesis that chimpanzees reared without their own mothers would be less competent socially, for example, by having fewer play or grooming partners, be less successful at initiating grooming, and so on.

Within any one zoo group, there were chimpanzees that had been brought up in very different ways but the zoos knew, for each individual, what it had experienced. If upbringing continued to affect social behaviour in later life, then this would have shown in persistent variation in adult behaviour, with the chimpanzees that had been reared by their own mothers being different from those that had been reared by humans or in a peer groups. In fact, this turned out not to be the case, and observations on the chimps when they were adults showed that there were few obvious effects of having been reared without a mother, although chimps reared by humans were slightly less successful at initiating social interactions than either the group-reared or mother-reared animals. This study shows how even in the absence of specific manipulation (no chimpanzees were deliberately removed from their mothers), the effects of early environment on adult behaviour can be studied using observations on existing groups of animals and without manipulating them in any way. Having to 'make do' with the groups of chimpanzees with very diverse histories who just happened to be living in five zoos, did not seem to be the ideal way to conduct research, but in fact it yielded very valuable data of direct use to zoos (section 7.2, 7.3).

2.5 Evolution (Phylogeny) of behaviour

We have now seen that questions of three different sorts—adaptation, causation, and development—can all be addressed through a purely observational approach, even though they all need different kinds of data to answer them. Questions about adaptation require us to think about how natural selection favours animals behaving in one way over those who do something different. Questions about causation require evidence about what stimulates a behaviour to happen in the here and now, or what makes an animal do one behaviour rather than another. Questions about development need evidence on the role of different factors in the upbringing of an animal on how it behaves as an adult. But Tinbergen (1963) also described a fourth kind of question, questions about evolution or phylogeny. What did he mean? What are phylogenetic questions about animal behaviour and how do they differ from the other three?

Questions about phylogeny are essentially about evolutionary origins—the behavioural equivalent of asking what horses' hooves evolved from, or what structure bats wings came from. They thus appear to be very difficult to answer because they refer to events that occurred many millions of years ago, effectively asking what the ancestors of bats looked like before they evolved proper wings. Both Niko Tinbergen and Konrad Lorenz attempted to answer questions about the phylogeny of behaviour by looking at a range of closely related living species and trying to work out whether one of them represented the 'ancestral state', Tinbergen on gulls (1959) and Lorenz on ducks (1958). For example, Lorenz pointed out that the sexual signals of some male ducks look a bit like preening movements and so possibly the signal evolved from preening. Ancestral male ducks preened their feathers, this may have attracted the attention of females, and so males that preened when females were around were more successful at mating. However, this was highly speculative and at the time (the 1950s and 1960s), there was no way of providing much evidence for such phylogenetic speculations. Then, with the advent of molecular techniques that measure the evolutionary distance between species and give 'family trees' of how closely related they are, the study of phylogeny took off in a big way. We can now ask questions about the evolutionary origins of behaviour and test hypotheses using molecular data.

For example, Summers et al. (2006) asked about the evolutionary origins of parental care in frogs and used a molecular approach to distinguish between different evolutionary scenarios. Frogs as a group show a huge range of reproductive strategies, ranging from species that care for their young by carrying them round on their backs (Fig. 2.8) to those that just lay their eggs and abandon them. Taking frogs as a whole, however, there is a correlation between egg size and degree of parental care. Those species that have the most parental care also have the largest eggs. The phylogenetic question here is: did parental care evolve first, allowing a 'safe harbour' that allowed the evolution of a smaller number of larger eggs that can then develop more slowly (Shine 1978), or did some frogs evolve large eggs first so that they had larger hatchlings which then lead to the evolution of better parenting to look after them?

Although this is a question about evolutionary events that took place a long time in the past, understanding the evolutionary relationships between living frog species allows us to reconstruct what is most likely to have happened. Molecular evidence now gives us a family tree of all frogs (Maddison, 2000) so we know which ones are closest to the first ancestral frog. Consider first what we should expect to see in living frogs if an increase in parental care preceded the evolution of larger egg and tadpole size (the safe harbour

Fig. 2.8   Male *Dendrobates* frog carrying his tadpole. Photograph by Jason Brown.

hypothesis). Evolution often leaves 'remnant' species along the wayside, so we could expect to find living examples of species that have small eggs and no parental care (the ancestral state), species that have large eggs and parental care (the evolved state), and a small number of remnant species that have small eggs and considerable parental care (halfway there). There should not, however, be species that have large eggs but no parental care as, on this hypothesis, this would not have been an evolutionary state any frogs went through. Now consider what we would expect on the alternative evolutionary scenario that an increase in egg size occurred before the evolution of parental care. If this is what happened, the halfway state would have been species with no parental care and large eggs, so there should still be some species around still showing this combination of traits. The 'missing group' should now be species that have small eggs but considerable parental care (Fig. 2.9).

The analysis done by Summers et al., showed that there are very few frogs that have the combination of small eggs and well developed parental care, which favours the first, safe harbour, hypothesis. The molecular evidence from the family trees of frogs suggests that what happened, apparently many different times in the past, is that species that had already evolved large egg size then evolved high levels of parental care to look after them.

Although such a study is now possible because a phylogeny of frogs based on DNA sequences has recently become available (Maddison, 2000), the basic

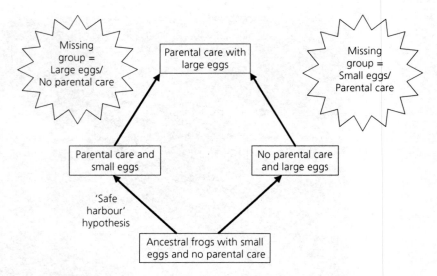

Fig. 2.9   Which came first, large eggs or increased parental care in frogs? If parental care came first, there should be no frogs with large eggs and no parental care. But if egg size increased first, followed by parental care, then the 'missing group' will be frogs with small eggs that look after their eggs.

units that went into the comparison were those derived from observational studies. Summers et al. had to rely on studies, done by other people, which had involved observing the breeding habits of many different species of frog to know which category to ascribe them to. If nobody had already done the basic observations and discovered which frog species do look after their offspring and which ones do not, the phylogenetic study would not have been possible. Once again, observation is essential.

2.6   Developing a hypothesis

It should now be clear why it is so important to know exactly which sort of question you are asking about animal behaviour. The question—adaptive, causal, developmental, or phylogenetic—determines the hypothesis that you decide to test, and the predictions of the hypothesis determine what kind of evidence you need to collect. Different kinds of question require, as we have seen, very different kinds of evidence to test them.

But the question 'What question are you asking?' now requires a more detailed answer than just 'A question about adaptation' or 'A question about development'. The answer needs to be phrased in terms of a specific hypothesis that can be tested with actual data. A general interest in the causation of foot-paddling, for instance, has to be turned into a hypothesis such as that foot-paddling is affected by the state of the tide, or the air temperature, or the numbers of other gulls also showing foot-paddling. Only once you have formulated a very specific hypothesis, and set out what its predictions are, can you begin to see what would count as evidence supporting the predictions and what would count against them. The pursuit deterrence hypothesis of stotting in gazelles (section 2.2.2) was tested through some very specific predictions about rates of stotting in gazelles picked out as victims and control animals running alongside them. The hydrodynamic theory of fish schooling (2.2.4) predicted precisely how far away from each other fish should swim.

Similarly, if you have hypothesized that gulls only foot-paddle at certain states of the tide, you need to test this by collecting data on the state of time and tides and observing the numbers of gulls foot-paddling, with the prediction that these should be correlated. If the hypothesis is correct, you should be able to find a correlation. If it is not correct, on the other hand, there should be no such correlation.

Do not take it as a sign of failure if you propose a hypothesis that then turns out to be wrong. What matters is how you have gone about formulating your hypotheses and whether your test of it is robust. In fact, vulnerability to being disproved by how real animals behave is the hallmark, not of a bad hypothesis, but of a good one (Chapter 8). The key to a good research project is to collect some new facts that no-one has thought of collecting before, so that you either expose the weakness of a hypothesis because it does not fit those new facts, or you add to its credibility because it can explain what happens in a new set of circumstances. Either way, you have made progress.

For this reason, defining your question in terms of a specific hypothesis with testable predictions is an essential next stage in any research project. Asking yourself: 'What question am I asking?' is both good discipline and very helpful in setting the 'story line' for the project report or research paper. You should state that you are testing a specific hypothesis by its predictions, which should be clearly listed in the introduction. Two or three predictions that are to be tested against your real observations will then allow the reader to follow the logic of your argument and understand the implications of your subsequent observations, whatever they show.

Predictions should be as specific as possible. Examples of good predictions that helpfully lend themselves to test would be a prediction that a particular behaviour (rate of pecking, say) is positively correlated with external temperature, with the number of other birds within one metre, or that rate of foot movements in foot-paddling gulls is related in a specified way to the properties of mud. Predictions expressed in such down to earth and basic terms give you a chance of being able to collect the data needed to test them one way or the other. Avoid predictions of the sort 'the animals should become more aggressive', unless you can say precisely what you are going to mean by 'aggressive' and how you are going to measure it. If you are unfamiliar with a particular animal and have no idea whether it ever is aggressive or what its aggressive behaviour looks like, don't worry. As we will see in Chapter 4, there is much to be said for spending a bit of time 'just watching' the animals to see what they actually do and allowing questions to arise in your mind. Tinbergen could never have asked his famous questions about why black-headed gulls remove egg shells (Tinbergen et al., 1962) if he hadn't been out there on the dunes watching the gull colony for other reasons and noticed this unexpected and transitory behaviour. Hypotheses are what science is about, but the hypotheses have got to come from somewhere. Ultimately, they come from observation.

2.7   From questions to answers

Once you have your hypothesis and have decided which of its predictions you are going to test, that is the time to design your observations, collect the data, and then analyse them statistically so that you have a clear answer about whether the predictions are upheld or not. Designing observations correctly is just as important as designing experiments correctly. And the statistical analysis of observational data is just as important as the analysis of experimental data, perhaps even more so, because of the greater danger from confounding variables and the wider range of statistical techniques that are open to us. There are, however, a range of decisions you have to make before you are ready to begin your observations, and it is these we will cover in the next chapters. These are such things as the numbers of animals you will need to observe, in what order, how you will choose them, what you are going to observe, and how you are going to record everything you want to. All these decisions will be crucial if you are to end up with a valid statistical analysis on the data you collect.

Don't worry if your understanding of statistical techniques is rudimentary, non-existent or, (which is much worse) confined to 'what comes out of a computer'. We are going to start at the very beginning so that you can see statistics in its proper place as an essential pattern-detecting tool, not as an incomprehensible no-go area. But the beginning, it may surprise you to learn, has nothing do with statistics or large sample sizes at all. The beginning is about observations that are so extraordinary and so unexpected that even with a sample size of one, they change our whole way of thinking about animals and point us all in completely new directions.

3 When all you need is one

Just before Christmas 1938, Marjorie Courtney-Latimer, the curator of the East London Museum in South Africa, went down to the nearby docks and climbed aboard one of the trawlers there, the *Nerine*. She had gone to wish seasons' greetings to the crew, who often gave her free specimens for her museum. That day, when she started to look through the pile of sharks, seaweed, and other marine life that the trawler had brought up, she noticed an unusual and very beautiful fish of a sort she had not seen before. It was about five feet long, mauve-blue with white spots, and it was iridescent all over. But the most extraordinary thing about it was that it had four limb-like fins and a strange wedge-shaped tail that she described as being like a puppy dog's.

The fish turned out to be a Coelacanth, thought at that time to have been extinct for at least 65 million years and known only from fossils (Fig. 3.1). Hailed internationally as one of the most sensational scientific discoveries of

Fig. 3.1   Model of a Coelocanth fish. Photograph by David Noakes.

the century, its scientific credentials were sealed by a publication in *Nature*. It was named *Latimeria chalumnae* J. L. B Smith, the *Latimeria* after its discoverer and J. L. B Smith denoting the person who formally identified and described it.

Just before Christmas 1952, the same J. L. B Smith received a telegram about another Coelacanth, this time caught off the Comoros Islands, half way between Mozambique and Madagascar. He initially described it as a different species (it was missing the first dorsal fin), and named it *Malania anjouani*, in honour of Malan, the Prime Minister of South Africa. The new species had been found in a completely different place and it, too, was described in a paper in *Nature*. And when another individual Coelacanth was landed in Manado Tua in Indonesia, it was called the scientific discovery of the decade and a third paper appeared in *Nature* in 1998.

So, here we have a case of no less than three papers in one of the most prestigious and respected scientific journals in the world, each paper based on a sample size of one. How does a sample size of one fit in with what statisticians tell us about needing many replicates to test any hypothesis? How can one coelacanth blow established scientific ideas out of the water all by itself when the foundation of good science seems to be that many independent replications are essential?

This chapter is about the power of the single observation—and why it is sometimes enough and why it is sometimes not. It is about when we should be impressed by one instance and when we are entitled to dismiss it as 'mere anecdote'. Understanding why single observations can sometimes be so powerful and at other times so inadequate is actually the key to understanding what the testing of scientific hypotheses is all about. It will help you to understand why there are occasions when the full armoury of statistical testing is needed so that, paradoxically, this chapter, with its emphasis on the value of the single observation, also paves the way for cases where the single observation on its own is almost useless. The key to understanding both is expectation. Science could, in fact, be described as Tales of the Expected or, to be more precise, the comparison between what a current hypothesis leads us to expect and what the real world actually comes up with.

Before 1938, the current view was that coelacanth fishes died out completely about 65 million years ago when there was a massive extinction of many other species, including the dinosaurs. The hypothesis that 'there are no living Coelacanths' was, therefore, refuted by one genuine specimen. Similarly, the hypothesis that 'Coelacanths only live off the coast of Africa' could be and was refuted by the discovery of a single fish captured off Indonesia. However, the hypothesis that South African coelacanths are larger than Indonesian coelacanths could not be refuted by a single individual from each place. If we had just two fish, then by chance, the single one from South Africa might be atypically large one and the one from Indonesia might be atypically small. Since it is impossible to establish the size of all the fish in both places, the only solution would be to measure a sample of several fish from each population and then to establish the relationship between the sample and the whole population. For this we do need more than two fish and the full barrage of statistics behind us.

In other words, one of the factors that determine whether or not a sample size of one is enough is—once again—exactly what hypothesis is being tested. Hypotheses of the form 'all xs are y' can be refuted by one counter-instance, whereas hypotheses of the form 'all xs are bigger/smaller/fatter/ more easily scared than y' (or even on average more) cannot be. This is because this second kind of hypothesis is making claims about impossibly large numbers of things such as all the women in the world or all the Coelacanths in Indonesian waters, which we would have no hope of being able to find or measure. For practical reasons, we have to make do with small samples and then infer what the whole lot would be like if we could measure them. The science of statistics is about guiding our inferences and telling us how confident we can be that we have learnt something about a very large number of animals when we have only looked at a very small sample of them. Obviously, we want to know whether the sample is representative of the whole population and with a sample size of one, we can't know whether or not it is. We will discuss the issue of how we know whether a sample is a good representative or not later (Chapter 6), but the point here is that for certain questions, such as whether Coelacanths or Thylacines (Tasmanian Wolves, also believed to be extinct), or Loch Ness Monsters exist, we aren't dealing with a sample. One animal alive or recently alive is enough.

We have to acknowledge, however, that the Coelacanth story has another ingredient that most single-case studies lack. This is the surprise or shock value of the discovery itself. Finding a pink shell in a species of snail previously thought to have only yellow-shelled individuals would violate the hypothesis that this species was always yellow, but it would hardly warrant a paper in *Nature* or cause much of a ripple outside the circle of dedicated malacologists who are interested in such things. It would fit in with what we know about colour variation in other species of snail. It would not violate the laws of genetics or evolution or what we know about pigmentation and camouflage.

But the Coelacanth did violate many expectations and much more dramat-ically. Against all the odds, it had survived without leaving any trace in the fossil record for about 65 million years (the date of the last known Coelacanth fossils)—a rather impressive 'gap' in the fossil record. It was also proposed (at least at the time of its discovery) to be an important missing link between fish and land animals—hence the title that J. L. B Smith gave to his book describing the history of its discovery—*Old Fourlegs* (1956). The shock value of finding it alive was considerable.

In the field of animal behaviour, too, single observations have caused shock waves and rethinks. Jane Goodall's (1968) observations on chimpanzees that we discussed in Chapter 1 showed that chimpanzees not only used tools but made them. A chimpanzee called David Greybeard showed her what chimpanzees could do and showed the rest of us that humans were no longer the only ape with technology.

More recently, the behaviour of single individual animals has again toppled the prevailing view about what animals can do. The widespread view that it was only primates that were capable of making their own tools has had to give way in the face of the achievements of a single New Caledonian crow named Betty. Betty made hooks to reach food she could not reach in any other way. When presented with food in a small bucket inside a cylinder (Fig. 3.2), Betty would take straight pieces of wire and bend one of the ends so that it formed a hook. She would then use her tool to reach down into the cylinder and put the hook under the handle of the bucket, which she could then pull up towards her (Weir et al., 2002). Because the previous beliefs (no non-primate can do make its own tools) were set up in such a clear-cut way, they were vulnerable to disproof by a single well-authenticated example of a non-primate—in this case a bird— doing what was supposed to be impossible.

Another bird, this time an African grey parrot called Alex, has also changed ideas about the cognitive abilities of animals. Alex has learnt to use English

Fig. 3.2   Betty the crow uses a hook that she made herself to reach a small bucket containing food. Photograph by Jackie Chappell.

words correctly, not just for objects like 'key' or 'cork', but also words for colours, shapes, and numbers (Pepperberg, 1999). If he is shown a set of three objects, even ones he has never seen before, and asked 'How many?' he will answer 'Three' or 'Three red'. Alex and Betty, as individual representatives of their species, have changed the meaning of the term 'bird brain' from dim-witted to something comparable to the best a chimpanzee can do. One crow and one parrot have changed what we consider the cognitive abilities of animals to be.

Dramatic observations that change the way people think do not, however, come often, and they do not come easily. Jane Goodall spent many months in the Gombe forests getting wild chimpanzees used to her presence before she saw her first instance of tool use. Christophe Boesch, who made equally dramatic discoveries about the way a mother chimpanzee teaches her offspring the skills of cracking nuts open with a pair of stones, spent over 20 years watching chimpanzees before seeing behaviour that could be considered to be evidence of teaching (Boesch, 1991). The first Coelacanth may have been discovered by chance, but the search for many of the others was long, very expensive, and full of disappointments. So the one dramatic observation that is going to change the way people think about the world is rare and is not recommended for undergraduate projects or even a PhD thesis. It is unlikely that you will be successful, at least if you rely on an unsystematic, needle-in-a-haystack approach, and hope that something will just turn up. You are very likely to find nothing at all and achieve nothing except to fail to find evidence for a hypothesis that everyone thought was very unlikely anyway. Fortunately, there is another way besides violating a deeply held belief that single observation research can achieve shock or surprise value and so establish its scientific credentials. This is by setting itself up in opposition to a range of alternative hypotheses and then showing that it is the only hypothesis that can explain the observed results. The surprise comes from being the one correct hypothesis among a crowd of incorrect ones. And it does this by being quantitative.

Think back to the kind of single observation we mentioned in the first chapter, where an astronomer predicts the exact hour on the exact day and in the exact place where a comet will appear—and it does. Here there are many of ways in which the astronomer could have been wrong, for example, by the comet appearing the year before, or the day before, or the hour after it was predicted. What impresses us about the astronomer's prediction is that the comet appears absolutely on time and that therefore he or she could so easily have been wrong. Because the prediction is quantitative (it states exactly when and where) rather than just stating that it will appear 'sometime in the next century', we have much more confidence in the underlying theory. There is still a surprise value if the prediction turns out to be correct, but it is not the shock of the new. We don't have to abandon any preconceived ideas and we don't have to revise the established laws of physics. On the contrary, the very precision of the prediction confirms that the current view that astronomers have of the way the solar system works is in fact correct. The shock is the shock of the quantitatively precise prediction being correct when it could so easily have been wrong. The theory 'sticks its neck out' by making such an accurate prediction and the reason we are impressed is because the more precise the prediction, the more likely it is that the theory is correct and that any other theory is wrong (Popper, 1959). The extent to which a theory makes unlikely predictions, which then turn out to be true, can even be calculated (Dawkins and Dawkins, 1969). For example, a theory that tells us exactly what hour a comet will appear is $100 \times 365 \times 24$ (876,000) times more likely to be wrong than a theory that simply tells us it will be 'sometime in the next century'. The 'sometime in the next century' hypothesis gives itself just one chance to be wrong (no comet appears during the specified 100 years). The quantitatively precise theory gives itself 875,999 chances to be wrong. That is why we are so impressed when it is right.

In the study of animal behaviour, too, precise predictions that distinguish different hypotheses also allow single observations to stand on their own. A beautiful example is a study of dragonfly flight by Adrian Thomas and his group. Dragonflies are high performance fliers. They can independently control their four wings to hover, accelerate in almost any direction, and manoeuvre at high speed. They are such good fliers that they can intercept and outmanoeuvre almost any other insect. One of their tricks is to use the lift generated by what are known as Leading Edge Vortices (LEVs)—eddies in the air generated on every downstroke of a wing. However, because they have two pairs of wings, they can also make use of the interactions produced by the vortices on different wings, rather in the way that helicopters make use of interactions between the different rotor blades. As you might imagine, this interaction is complex and it was not well understood until Thomas et al. (2004) started to analyse what was going on by actually observing the vortices coming off the wings. They did this by observing free-flying dragon-flies and making the vortices show up by releasing tiny jets of smoke. As a dragonfly flew up the smoke stream, its flight perturbed the smoke particles and showed up all the disturbances in the air that its flight was causing. (Of course, everything happens at very high speed, so they were not observing with the naked eye but with very high speed video cameras).

What Thomas et al. wanted to know was exactly how the potentially unsteady and erratic pattern of airflow generated by four fast moving wings was translated into the controlled super-flight of a hunting dragonfly. They considered three hypotheses that were all derived from classical aerodynamic analysis of complex jet streams, but the three hypotheses made completely different predictions about what should happen as air moves over and under a dragonfly wing during a downstroke. These predictions are explained in more detail in Fig. 3.3. The important point is that although each hypothesis invokes Leading Edge Vortices as providing the lift in dragonfly flight, they differ in the quantitative details of exactly how lift is achieved.

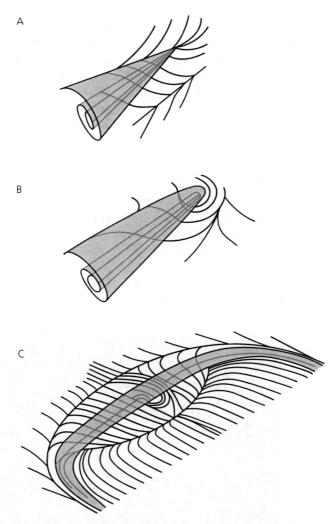

Fig. 3.3 Three hypotheses about how lift is achieved in dragonfly flight. On the first hypothesis (Fig. 3.3A), there should be a bifurcation of the air with separation of the overwing and underwing streams, each moving away from the wing surface. On the second hypothesis (Fig. 3.3B), there should be an unsteady region near the end of the wing, and on the third there should be a simple U-shaped separation (Fig. 3.3C). Each of these hypotheses invokes LEVs. They differ in the details of how these are employed in flight. (From Thomas et al., 2004).

Observations of how smoke particles actually move over the surface of a dragonfly wing, showed that they extended continuously over the centre of the dragonfly's thorax in the U-shaped pattern predicted by the third hypothesis (Fig. 3.4). Such an observation ruled out the other two hypotheses because their predictions were so different. Even one high quality set of pictures of one dragonfly in flight was enough to distinguish between the hypotheses, but this was only possible because the predictions were clearly distinguishable from one another. If the predictions had just been of the form 'the air should flow faster' or 'there should be a vortex somewhere', the single observation would not have been sufficient to discriminate between them. Each theory stuck its neck out and made predictions about the detailed pattern of air flow. The intricate and beautiful patterns seen in the real dragonfly matched the predictions of the third theory so closely and so clearly that we can accept the single observation as a valid test on its own.

There are thus two conditions when single observations or sample sizes of one animal are all that is necessary to draw valid conclusions. These are:

1) When testing hypotheses of the form 'all xs are y' or 'no xs are y'. One counter-instance will be enough to show the hypothesis is false, provided, of course, that it is well authenticated. You will not get away with claiming to have seen a reputedly extinct animal without providing very good evidence indeed.
2) When you are testing intrinsically surprising predictions from quantitatively precise theories. The predictions you test should be unlikely in the

Fig. 3.4   Dragonfly flying in a stream of smoke to reveal the vortices coming off the back of the wing. The pattern is clearly more similar to the U-shaped pattern predicted in Fig. 3(C) than to either of the other hypotheses. Photograph by Richard Bomphrey.

sense of being vulnerable to being proved wrong and so clearly distinct from those of other hypotheses. They should ideally be pitted against those of other competing explanations to see which one best fits real data.

Many of the questions we want to ask about animal behaviour, however, do not lend themselves to either of these forms, and therefore need to be tested in other ways. They require much more than one observation and usually many more than one animal. They involve questions about the way things are in the world, such as whether males of a given species are more aggressive than females, or whether South African coelacanths are more likely to hide in crevices than Indonesian ones. A single instance here could be positively misleading. One highly aggressive female doesn't show that all females are more aggressive than all males in that species. She might be unusually large, or unusually hungry, or had an unusual upbringing, quite atypical for her sex. Where we want to make predictions about whole groups of animals or to understand the behaviour of whole species, we need an altogether different approach, one that includes not just the observations we have actually been able to make, but an indication of how typical or representative of the whole group or species those observations are. We need to record not one but many instances in a carefully planned way, and we need to make our observations with a clear idea of how we are going to analyse them later on. As with the design of experiments, the design of observations determines to a very large extent how valid the results ultimately turn out to be. No amount of clever statistical analysis will cover up badly done or badly planned observations, any more than it will cover up badly done or badly planned experiments. In fact, as we will see in the next chapter, the principles of good observational design are almost exactly the same as those of good experimental design. In both cases, we have to make sure that our samples (that is, the data we can physically collect in the time available) are a fair representation of the real world. In both cases, good design is the key to making sure that they are.

4 Three principles of observational design

We now turn to research that does not fall into the 'one observation that will change the world' category. You have not trapped the Loch Ness Monster, nor discovered a mouse that speaks perfect Hebrew, nor even derived a precise mathematical theory of how your animals should behave, but let us suppose that you have formulated some sort of a hypothesis. This hypothesis is most likely to be of the form 'x increases (or decreases) behaviour y'. You will thus almost certainly need to make more than one observation, probably whole sets of observations. In fact, because animal behaviour tends to be so variable, you will probably need a very large number of observations indeed. This is something that cell biologists and others who do not have to grapple constantly with variation in their animals, often do not understand. You may even find them making disparaging remarks about research that is, in their view, so badly designed that it *needs* statistics. Their experiments, they will tell you, work the same way every time, so they only need to do things once.

Animal behaviour is fundamentally different. Not only do animals of the same species behave differently from each other, but what the same animal does on different occasions can be affected by a host of different factors, some of which you may be able to identify, such as the time of day or the weather, and some of which you cannot. The result is that sometimes the animals behave in one way and sometimes they do something completely different and you may have no idea why. This means that if you want to know whether their behaviour is affected by something you are particularly interested in, such as whether they are alone or in a group, you have to *design* your observations in such a way that you can infer that it is their social environment that is causing the effect and not just that they are having a bad hair day or that they have just been disturbed by the sound of gunshot.

Good design in the way data is collected is as important for observation as it is for actual experiment. Grafen and Hails (2002) refer to the three principles of good experimental design as replication, randomization, and blocking. In this chapter we will see that the same three principles apply just as much to an observational study as they do to an experimental one. Even though the animals themselves may not be controlled experimentally, the observer has the power to control the way he or she makes observations. To make it easier to see what the three principles mean for observational studies in practice, I shall refer to them by their slightly fuller names of Independent Replication, Not Confounding Variables, and Removing Known Sources of Variation. Whatever their names, if you keep to them, you will be able to draw valid inferences from what you observe animals to be doing. If you ignore them, your data, although voluminous and painstakingly collected, will have very little value.

4.1   Principle 1: Independent replication

'Replication' means having a sufficient number of independent observations or replicates. The key here is the word 'independent', and understanding what it means in this rather unusual context is fundamental to understanding the basis of statistical reasoning. Consider the classic example of tossing a coin to see if it is biased. You want to test the hypothesis that your coin has a tendency to come down head upwards more often than you would expect 'by chance'.

You toss the coin once. It spins, clatters to the floor and lies there head upwards. Obviously, if this happens once, it does not show that your coin is biased towards heads because even a completely unbiased coin would have a 50:50 chance of coming up heads the first time you tossed it. So far, a biased and an unbiased coin would not be expected to have produced noticeably different results. Now, suppose someone comes up with a crazy suggestion. They suggest that instead of tossing the coin several more times, it should be left where it fell. Then, at minute intervals, the two of you should record whether the head was still visible. After an hour of this, there would be 60 cases of 'heads' and zero of 'tails', quite enough, he explains, to show that the coin is biased because 60:0 is bound to be 'significant'.

The lunacy of this suggestion should be obvious: the once-tossed coin has not been given enough chances to show whether it is biased or not. For that, it needs to be tossed many independent times. If it remains untouched, its position in one minute is entirely predictable (dependent) on its position a minute earlier. Come to that, if you recorded its position every second instead of once a minute, you would end up an hour later with a figure of 3,600 heads and no tails—even more significant odds, if you are prepared to swallow the crazy logic. Whenever you can increase the apparent odds merely by altering the time interval between measurements, you should suspect that you might have committed the primary error of non-independence: one data point being predictable from another.

4.1.1 Independence in animal behaviour

Although the example of tossing a coin once and leaving it there is (I hope) obviously flawed, it is surprising how easily very similar mistakes can slip into examples of animal behaviour. If you were studying where starlings prefer to roost, for example, you might decide to study one large flock consisting of several thousand birds. One night you observe the entire flock settling under a large suspension bridge just as darkness falls. The obvious pitfall would be to record whether the flock was still there one hour, two hours, three hours and four hours later and believe that you had four data points, because, like the coin, the starlings have made one decision, settled down and are extremely unlikely to change halfway through the night. But there are other sources of non-independence here too. If there were 10,000 birds, you cannot claim that starlings have an overwhelming preference for roosting under bridges on the grounds that 10,000 of them chose the bridge and 0 did not, because the behaviour of one starling is highly dependent on that of the others. Starlings copy each other. They do not roost alone, and if several have chosen the bridge, then the rest will probably follow suit. So even with that many birds, there is really only one independent decision to roost under a bridge. For one flock making one choice, n (the number of independent replicates) = 1.

But what if you went back night after night and found that the flock still roosted under the same bridge? Isn't flying away during the daytime and coming back again at night the equivalent of tossing a coin? Couldn't you say, after 10 nights of the same behaviour, that you had 10 independent choices for roosting under a bridge and none for roosting elsewhere? Unfortunately not, because animals have memories (which coins do not), and because their behaviour is often dependent on what they did the night before. This means that retesting and re-observing the same animals on different occasions is not as independent as separate coin tosses. Sometimes this memory-based type of non-independence is reasonably easy to spot. For example, if a mouse goes along the same path night after night, it could be following an odour trail which it then revitalizes with fresh urine each night. Its behaviour on one night would then be highly dependent on what it did the night before. In the case of starling flocks, this dependence may be less obvious because the starlings are not following odour trails but, like humans going home every evening to the same house, the starlings are creatures of habit and, once having found a reasonable roost site, they are more likely to return to it out of inertia or just because it is familiar. They no more make completely independent decisions about where to roost every evening than people make completely different decisions about where to live every day.

To be on the safe side, the independent statistical unit here should be the whole flock of starlings. By all means, follow them for several nights to see if they are consistent and always go to the same place, but in your study of starling roosting preferences, enter just one observation for that flock, either 'under bridge', or '8/10 nights under bridge' because you so far have only one independent observation (one flock). To increase your sample size get on the phone or the internet and find as many other different flocks of starlings in different parts of the country as you can. If they, too, roost under bridges, then your conclusions become much more valid because your independent sample size has increased.

So, in the study of animal behaviour, we constantly have to be on the look out for hidden sources of non-independence such as animals influencing each other, being influenced by what they themselves did on a previous occasion, or falsely inflated data sets that contain the equivalent of repeated observations on unmoving coins. *Pseudo-replication* is the name given to using data sets that appear to be independent replicates when in fact there are hidden sources of non-independence that make the whole set invalid.

This does not mean, however, that we must only ever observe one animal once to be sure of avoiding pseudo-replication. As we will see later in this chapter, (section 4.4) there can be some very good reasons for observing the same animals repeatedly and one of the most important of these to make sure that the observations give a typical representation of behaviour. Free-range chickens are much more likely to come out of their houses in the early morning and evening than they are at midday (Dawkins et al., 2003) so measuring ranging behaviour once a day at noon could give a very misleading impression of how much the birds use their range areas. Repeated observations on the same flocks throughout the day are positively needed to give a full picture of range use. The repeated observations should not be used to inflate the sample size, which should still remain as the number of independent flocks. All that changes with repeated observations throughout the day is that the data from each flock becomes more accurate. The mean number of birds seen outside, based on twelve hourly observations made throughout the whole day, is a more accurate measure of range use than just the number seen outside during a single observation period at midday.

Although independence is an ideal and you should always aim to have as much of it as possible, it is not always a single obtainable goal. It is like climbing a mountain where the summit appears to be in view but when you get there, it turns out to be just a ridge and the real summit is still above you. You just have to make things as independent as you possibly can. For example, suppose you discovered a second flock of starlings not very far away from the first that also roosted under a very similar bridge. This looks like two independent 'bridge' decisions but what if the second flock turned out to be an offshoot of the first with many members having spent their formative early months roosting under the same bridge as the first before they split and formed a separate flock? The persistence of the bridge-roosting habit in the second flock makes them more independent of the first than if you had studied two birds within the same flock, but not as independent as if you had chosen two flocks that had no possible connection with each other. However, you have to call a halt somewhere because the quest for total independence is probably an endless one. All the starling flocks in the country might have some possible links if you looked hard enough. The best advice is to achieve as much independence as you possibly can and be very conservative in what you take as your independent statistical unit. Even though condensing your many observations into a single mean per flock or herd may make you feel as though you are throwing away a lot of valuable data, the independence you achieve will make the data much more valid and you will have gone a long way to avoiding the dangers of pseudo-replication.

4.1.2 Statistical independence v. biological validity

But there is a problem. If the search for independence means dividing up your available animals into different groups so that they become 'different' independent units rather than a single unit, this can itself lead to results that, although statistically valid, cease to be biologically valid. This problem is so serious and so unrecognized that we cannot leave this discussion of independence without understanding the delicate balance between these two types of validity.

As we have just seen, one of the key elements of statistical validity is independence of the data points. Now, suppose we have a flock of 20 sheep and we want to find out whether sheep respond differently to large dogs or small dogs. If we kept the flock as a group of 20, we would only have one flock $(n = 1)$ and the behaviour of all of the sheep would be highly dependent on that of the other sheep in the group. So, to avoid pseudo-replication, we divide the sheep up into 20 separate pens and test 10 with a large dog and 10 with a small dog. We test the sheep as singletons and congratulate ourselves on now having a reasonable sample size (sample size of group with small dog $n_1 = 10$; sample size of group with large dog $n_2 = 10$). We might even find a statistically significant difference between the two groups.

The trouble is that although statistically reasonable, such an experiment/ observation would be biologically meaningless. Sheep do not go around as singletons. They are flock animals and behaviour of isolated animals is therefore atypical, abnormal, and probably that of a distressed animal. This means that you have to be extremely careful to make sure that, in achieving statistical independence, you have not sacrificed something more important— namely valid answers to the questions of interest. So if you want to know how sheep respond to dogs, don't use isolated animals because you will learn little of value to a sheep farmer, or indeed a biologist interested in the behaviour of animals evolved to live in groups. It would be much better to keep sheep in larger, more natural groups, have a smaller sample size on this farm and go in search of other farms with more sheep to increase your sample size.

All too often in the history of applied research, results that are perfectly valid statistically have never found their way into practical application in the real world, at least partly because they were done on small groups of chickens or pigs to ensure proper replication and independence of data. They thereby lost all connection with real-world farming where group sizes are often incomparably larger. What is true for groups of 20 chickens or 200 may have little bearing on what happens on commercial farms where groups of 20,000 or more are common. The result is that some scientific work, although statistically impeccable, may not be seen as relevant to the real world. So it is important to aim for both independence *and* validity. Think big. Think of replicating your results in different places, with totally different animals, so that a whole zoo or farm or coral reef becomes your independent unit of replication (Chapter 7). Go to coral reefs on lots of different islands. Go to different farms. Be ultraconservative with your data, emerging with a single conglomerate observation for one place and not being seduced by the idea that just because you can see lots of animals, you necessarily have more than one independent reading. That way, you avoid pseudo-replication and at the same time you produce valid results.

Incidentally, the more observant among you may have noticed that yet another source of non-independence crept into one of our examples. If we want to know whether sheep respond differently to large dogs (plural) compared to small dogs, we should not use the same two dogs for all our observations. If we had a little yappy dog and a large strong silent one, the sheep might be responding more to the particular dog than to its size. So even though we might have enough independent flocks of sheep to be able to say that we had satisfied the requirements of independence for the sheep side of the study, we could still be guilty of pseudo-replication if we used the same two dogs each time. We could strictly speaking only say that the sheep responded differently to those two individual dogs. If we wanted to make more general statements about their responses to large and small dogs, we would need to use a wider range of dogs as our stimuli.

The reason that statisticians give such priority to independence of data is that all their statistical tests are based on working out the probability that something would happen 'by chance' when that chance is based on independent events—the animal behaviour equivalents of independent coin tosses. If your results are non-independent—various versions of staring at untouched coins—all their tables and p values are useless. Unbiased coins do sometimes come up with runs of 10 heads in a row even when tossed perfectly fairly.

Monkeys at typewriters do sometimes produce words and even sensible phrases. To work out how likely this is to happen by chance, statisticians *assume* independence of each coin toss or monkey key press. Independence is the basis of statistics and if you want to be able to apply statistics to your data, you have to make sure you also have achieved independence. If you toss a coin 1,000 times and it still shows 1,000 heads and no tails, then you really would have to believe it is a biased coin: the probability of that happening by chance is so low as to be almost negligible. But you can only work out what that probability is on the assumption that each coin toss is fairly conducted and that an unbiased coin tossed in the same way would have a 50% chance of showing a head and a 50% chance of showing tails each time it flew into the air. Each and every toss starts from scratch with exactly the same chance of going either way. This is the way research has to be designed as well, because this is the only way in which discrepancies from chance can be detected.

We can now see why replication is so necessary. For the first few tosses, the behaviour of the unbiased coin and that of the biased one will not be distinguishable. It is only as the coin tossing continues and it becomes less and less likely that the genuinely unbiased one will continue to match the regular sequences of heads that the biased one is producing, that we begin to be confident of 'bias'. The more independent replications we have, the clearer will be the discrepancies from chance.

4.2 Principle 2. Not confounding variables (by randomization and other means)

A big danger with both observations and experiments is that what you think is causing an effect is not in fact what is causing it (section 1.5), because of what are called *confounding variables*. For example, suppose you concluded that, for a particular species, males were more active than females. They ran about more, moved around more, spent less time lying down, and so on. But suppose you had observed the males in the morning and the females in the afternoon. You could not know whether your results were due to the fact that males really were more active, or because all members of that species—males and females—were more active in the morning than in the afternoon. If that were the way you had carried out your observations, sex and time of day would have been completely *confounded*, or so completely mixed up together that you could not possibly disentangle them. This would be such a bad design that it could not be rescued by statistics.

The obvious way round this is to make sure that you observe both males and females in the morning and the afternoon. That way, even though both sexes may be more active in the morning, you could still legitimately identify a sex difference. If both were more active in the morning, but the males were even more active, you would still be able to disentangle (unconfound) the influence of sex and time of day.

Note that 'unconfounding' is not the same as 'getting rid of altogether'. Nothing is going to alter the fact that these animals may be more active in the morning than in the afternoon, however much you try to keep everything else constant. Perhaps there is more traffic on a nearby road in the afternoons. Perhaps it is hotter. Perhaps there are other differences between your observation sessions that you have not even thought of, such as variation in the numbers of aircraft flying overhead, or even variation in your own vigilance as an observer depending on how tired you are. In other words, there will inevitably be a large range of factors, some of which you are aware of and some of which you are not, that could affect the behaviour of your animals in addition to the one (such as whether they are males or females) that you have decided to investigate. But while it is inevitable that such factors will be there and will continue to affect the behaviour of the animals throughout your study, it is not inevitable that you have to let them *confound* your results. By taking some simple steps in the way you design your observations, you can very convincingly disentangle the effects of these unwanted factors from the differences between males and females. The secret is to make quite sure that all the other factors have an equal chance of affecting the behaviour of both males and females.

For example, by making sure that you observe equal numbers of males and females at both times of day, the effects of time of day will fall equally on both sexes. If there is still a difference between males and females, you can believe that it is a genuine difference between the sexes because it is showing up *despite* the possible differences due to time of day. You will be comparing like with like: males versus females in the morning and males versus females in the afternoon. Males observed in the morning versus females observed in the afternoon are not like for like, and totally confound sex and time of day.

Making sure equal numbers of males and females are observed at each time of day by alternating your observations (observing a male, then a female, then switching back to another male, and so on) is perhaps the most obvious way of designing valid observations, but you should be aware that statisticians prefer you to go one step further. They want you to randomize.

4.2.1 Randomizing, alternating and balancing

Statisticians love random numbers for the simple reason that randomness is the opposite of order and pattern. So if you decided to observe the behaviour of 20 males and 20 females for 20 minutes each, spread across a day, a statistician might suggest that you should randomize the order of observing males and females, so that nothing else could confound the difference between the sexes. If you observed in a non-random way—such as alternating between observing a male at the beginning of every hour and females on the half hour—it is just possible that your results could be confounded with something else happening in the environment. Perhaps a noisy machine switches itself on and off for half an hour every hour, and you happen to observe males when the machine comes on and females half an hour later when the machine is off but don't notice the effect the machine is having on the animals. If you alternated your observations throughout the day on the half hour (9 am: Male, 9.30: Female, 10 am: Male, 10.30: Female etc...) you could inadvertently be confounding differences between the sexes with machine activity. You might have unconfounded sex and time of day, but the coincidence between the machine switching on and off and your observation periods would then have confounded sex and the effects of the machine. But by randomizing your observations, any regularity or pattern in the environment—whether or not you had thought of it—would be decoupled from your systematically observed differences between males and females. Choosing to observe males and females in random order throughout the day takes care of everything else—time of day, aircraft, loud noises, machines, and sleepy observers.

There is just one snag with random numbers in practice. They can sometimes—completely by chance—lead to sequences of the same type of observation. For example, am: Male, Male, Male, Female, pm: Male, Female, Female, Female is a possible random sequence for observing four males and four females, but one that just could happen to end up with most of the males being observed in the morning and most of the females in the afternoon, the very thing we wanted to guard against. Even alternation would be better than this.

One solution is not to randomize but to *balance*—that is, to make sure that equal numbers of observations on males and females take place in the morning and the afternoon, but to break the strict alternation by making sure that as many female observations occur before as after males ones. A balanced order might be am: MFFM; pm: MFFM. In this way, time of day is 'balanced' across the sexes, as is the tiredness of the observer, and any other possible effects of the order in which observations are made. It also solves most of the other problems of confounding variables even though it lacks the purity of a random sequence. (A really fussy statistician could still argue that some hitherto undetected factor was also managing to balance in step with our balanced observations, but the account of what this factor might conceivably be would become more and more fantastic). Certainly for many behavioural experiments, balancing is preferable in practice to strict randomization, because of the non-random looking sequences that can come out of a random number generator for small numbers. Balancing is a pragmatic solution that allows you to deal with the variables that are most likely to be confounded with the effects you want to show, and at the same time gives you results that will be statistically valid. Most statisticians will accept this as a compromise.

4.2.2 Choice of animals and of observers

So far, we have only considered the importance of making sure there are no confounding variables as far as the *order of making observation* is concerned, but we have to be just as careful to avoid a host of other potential confounding variables. Chief of these are the choices of *which animals to observe* and *the way in which observers are allocated* to which animals.

When designing an experiment with two or more treatments, attention obviously has to be paid to the choice of which animals go into which treatment group, so that not all the big fat confident animals get treatment A and all the smaller ones that hover in the background get B, because then any apparent differences between A and B will be confounded by the personality differences between animals. With observational design this problem is just as acute, if not more so, as it is all too easy to have your eye caught by the cute little animal on the left or the active one in the centre of your view. If males are more distinctive and more widely separated than females, you might inadvertently choose a male to observe because he happened to be close to you and curious enough to approach you, thereby causing you to choose a particularly active male. Alternatively (because you were testing the hypothesis that females were more sedentary) you might unconsciously choose a small female who happened to be sitting down for your next observation. I don't mean that you would consciously cheat (although someone who wanted to challenge your conclusions might accuse you of doing so) but it is a wise precaution to choose random animals to observe, and this goes as much for animals caught on video or CCTV as it does for those you are observing directly. Fortunately, there are some easy ways of doing this.

One of the simplest is to take a sheet of clear acetate on which there are gridlines dividing the whole sheet into squares. Number the rows and columns and choose a random number. Do this using a random number table (Appendix 1), the random number generator on a computer, or, you do not have access to any of these, use dice or numbers out of a hat. Note down the grid square that corresponds to this random number. If you are analysing videotapes, place the acetate sheet up against the monitor screen and choose the animal closest to the centre of your chosen grid square. If you are observing live animals, hold the grid square vertically at arm's length and do the

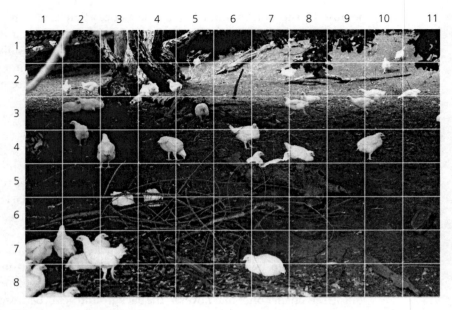

Fig. 4.1   The acetate sheet method for choosing a random animal from a group. Using a two digit random number, choose the animal closest to that square to observe.

same (Fig. 4.1). Keep your eye on the selected animal, even though it may not appear, at the time, to be doing very much. That is the randomly chosen animal you should then observe.

If more than one person is going to be making the observations, you will also need to ensure that observers themselves do not introduce yet another confounding effect into the results. Even if all the observers have agreed on how they are going to record behaviour, there is always the possibility that there will be differences in the record from different observers, or in the ways the animals being observed react to them. If one enthusiastic observer who has trouble sitting still is assigned to record the behaviour of males and another more cautious, quieter observer is told to observe females, you could get a serious confounding of genuine sex differences with observer differences.

Given that you may sometimes have to rely on more than one observer for logistical or practical reasons, you need to give some thought to how best to eliminate such observer bias. Training or practice is essential if more than one of you is going to observe, and checking one observer against another to ensure that you are both recording the same things in the same way is a useful precaution (section 6.9). It is also good practice to randomly assign observers to different groups of animals or to make sure that each observer has observed the same number of animals in each group in a balanced way.

As a further precaution against observer bias, you may want to go even further and arrange that the observers do not know what differences between the animals there might be. For example, suppose you wanted to know whether having been a twin or a singleton made a difference to the behaviour of a sheep when it was grown up. You set up a study in which the observations are carried out by people who do not know at the time when they do the observations which sheep were twins and which were not. Each observer is just told to record the behaviour of sheep with particular numbers on them, without knowing what the numbers stand for. This would completely eliminate the possibility that the observations could be inadvertently biased by someone who was already convinced that having been reared with a twin made a sheep more docile, or more active, or whatever pet hypothesis they might be nursing.

Conducting your observations 'blind' in this way is an ideal but not always possible. For example, you couldn't really be blind to the fact that you were watching a male elephant rather than a female elephant, or a stag rather than a hind, but do your best. Try to think through your research design with the eyes of a critical referee and see if a case could be made for your results being confounded with any other factor, including observer bias.

At this point, you can probably see why so many scientists prefer 'experiments' that allow actual manipulation of the world to 'observations' that force you take what happens to be there. It appears to be so much easier to unconfound your variables and to separate correlation from causation if you can actively move things around in the world. Causing something to happen when and where you want it seems so much more definitive and watertight than 'just watching'. But by now, you should be able to see that observation is not nearly as passive a process as appears at first. You may not be controlling your animals, but you are in control of where and how you make your observations. You substitute discipline over your own observations for manipulation of your animals (Altmann, 1974). Of course, as we have seen throughout this book, you may eventually decide that you need to do an experiment as the final test of your hypothesis. But much can be done before you reach the point of the final 'clincher' experiment. Good observational design can unconfound many of the same variables as an actual experiment would do, only without disturbing the animals as much.

4.3   Principle 3. Removing known sources of variation by blocking or matching

The third important element of both observational and experimental design is 'blocking' (sometimes called matching). Blocking is an extension of the idea of comparing 'like with like' to remove confounding variables (section 4.1) and is an immensely powerful way of using statistics to remove unwanted sources of variation from your data. However, blocking is both widely misunderstood and misapplied, so it is necessary for us to take a little time to understand why it is so important.

The starting point—a pretty obvious one—is that if you want to be able to show up an effect of something either experimentally or through observations, you are most likely to be able to do this if you keep all other sources of variation in your data as low as possible. For example, if you wanted to see whether variations in what people eat has an effect on their mood, you would be most likely to show such an effect if you chose to look at people of the same sex, age, natural body weight, and so on. If the people you were studying were very variable to start with, for example young army recruits and old age pensioners, or included some very obese or some very thin people, any effects of food on mood state might well get swamped by all this other variation. This obvious fact is the reason why so many scientists—for instance those wanting to see if one drug is more effective than another—demand genetically similar animals of the same age and sex, reared in exactly the same conditions. If they keep unexplained or background variation to a minimum, they are most likely to get a significant effect of what they are interested in (Chapter 8).

So, on the face of it, it would seem that research should be done by keeping everything as much the same as you can, except for the one variable you are interested in. In the study of animal behaviour, however, this is often not possible and for some of the questions we ask, it isn't even desirable. One of the reasons for this is that background or unwanted variation is often a fact of life. Real animals, living in zoos, or on farms, or in the wild, are unlikely to be genetically identical and they will not necessarily have been reared in the same way. You cannot order a batch of genetically identical giraffes just for your research in the way you can order identically reared, genetically similar mice. So rather than trying to eliminate background or unwanted variation in your animals, you may have to learn to live with it and even actually make use of it to tell you some extra things about your animals. Zoos, after all, want to know about giraffes in general, not necessarily just one genetic strain.

There are two main ways of doing this. The first, which we have already dealt with, is to use randomization or balancing (section 4.2.2). Even if there is a lot of unavoidable background variation, randomized or balanced designs help to ensure that it does not *confound* the main conclusions. The second is *blocking*. Since much of the terminology of statistics comes from its development within an agricultural setting, we will use the example of growing crops in a field to illustrate exactly what blocking means.

Many of the statistical tests we use today were developed at Rothampstead Experimental Station by Sir Ronald Fisher to answer questions such as whether one particular variety of cereal yielded more grain than another. Fisher (1925, 1935) designed his statistical tests to deal with situations where there was unavoidable variation (such as different soil types or drainage) in different parts of a field, and yet people wanted to know whether there were genuine differences between the varieties. This means that his tests are very well suited to the study of animal behaviour where background variation is also an unavoidable fact of life. The sort of situation he dealt with was where there might be only one field available for growing different varieties of a cereal, but that field was not uniform. It might have a noticeable slope with heavy, often wet ground at the bottom and a more exposed, drier and winder area at the top. Obviously, one variety of barley, A, should not be grown at the top of the field, and variety B on the bottom, as this would make it impossible to separate the effects of variety from those due to position in the field. One possible approach would have been to divide the entire field into small areas or 'plots' and then either randomly assign the different varieties to different plots across the field, or balance the plots so that there were equal numbers of plots with each variety in the high and low parts of the field. This is the approach we discussed under Principle 2 and it would be a perfectly reasonable way of comparing the effects of two or more varieties of barley. However, Fisher devised a system that gave even more information from the same sized field. Furthermore, he showed how it was possible to compare not just two varieties, but several all at the same time.

Fisher kept the idea of small plots, some of which would be sown with one variety and some of which would be sown with another, but instead of randomly assigning the different varieties to the different plots, or even alternating or balancing, he systematically grouped plots together into larger units or 'blocks'. Thus an entire field would be divided into these blocks and each block would be divided into plots. Within each block, there would be a random allocation of plots to varieties. Fig. 4.2 illustrates Fisher's Randomized Block design for comparing the yields of four varieties of barley within a very non-uniform field.

The field is divided into eight blocks and within each block are four plots, one allocated to each of the four varieties of barley A–D. Within a block, fertilizer treatments are randomly assigned to the four plots.

If the field slopes, some of the blocks will be at the top of the hill, some at the bottom, and some in between. Because the blocks might be subject to different soil or drainage, it is to be expected that there would be differences *between* the blocks. But *within* a block, the A, B, C, and D plots are directly comparable because they have similar soil types and drainage. Each block thus constitutes a mini-experiment of its own, and the same mini-experiment is then replicated all over the field: like is thus compared to like. However, as well as ensuring that we do not confound variables (such as variety with field elevation), we also have some very valuable additional information. Comparison *between* different blocks, or mini-experiments in different parts of the field, tells us whether a block's position within the field does in

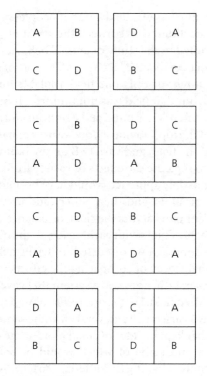

Fig. 4.2 A randomized block design.

fact have an effect on plant growth. Blocking thus gives two sorts of information in one experiment. It tells us about the yields of the different varieties (A versus B versus C versus D within each block) and it also tells us about how the yield of each variety varies with position in the field (comparison between blocks). It could be very valuable to know that, say, A gives better results than B when the soil is damp, but that the difference is even more pronounced in the plots are on the drier, higher ground.

But from a statistical point of view, differences between blocks are even more important because they allow us to effectively get rid of a lot of unwanted background variation (that due to the different soil types in the different parts of the field) and so allow the yields of the different varieties of barley to become even more obvious. It may sound rather odd to say we can get rid of variation statistically, but it was Fisher's genius to realise that we can do just that. If we know how large this unwanted variation between blocks is, we can effectively disregard it. But the only way we can be sure we have correctly measured the background variation is to use blocking. We do the same experiment in every bit of the field and so we know what effects there are due to position. By blocking, we turn a variable sloping field into a

A

BLOCK 1	BLOCK 2	BLOCK 3	BLOCK 4
1 Male	1 Male	1 Male	1 Male
2 Female	2 Female	2 Female	2 Female
3 Female	3 Female	3 Female	3 Female
4 Male	4 Male	4 Male	4 Male

B

BLOCK 1	BLOCK 2	BLOCK 3	BLOCK 4
1 Male	1 Male	1 Female	1 Female
2 Female	2 Female	2 Male	2 Male
3 Female	3 Male	3 Female	3 Male
4 Male	4 Female	4 Male	4 Female

Fig. 4.3 Two possible designs for the observations on males and females. Both designs use blocking, but A shows a design balanced for test order within each block, with as males tested before and after females, and with the same order in each block. B, on the other hand, varies the order between blocks. There are advantages and disadvantages to different designs, which are discussed in most statistical texts.

completely uniform one but not by physically imposing uniformity on a real field. Rather, we statistically remove the known effects of different parts of the field, so leaving it effectively uniform.

If you want to understand the statistical reasoning behind this power of blocking, you should turn a more mathematical account such as that found in Grafen and Hails (2002, p.80). The key test is called the Analysis of Variance, invented by Fisher to extract the maximum information and statistical significance from blocked designs. We will encounter the Analysis of Variance later, when we come to how you might analyse your results (Chapter 8), but don't worry if you are one of those people who hate anything statistical or mathematical. All you need to know at this stage is that blocking is a very important design principle that, if you adopt it, can only help you in collecting good data.

Blocking is just as powerful an aid to observational design as it is to the design of the agricultural experiments it was originally developed for, but it has to be said that the definition of a 'block' has become somewhat stretched. It no longer has to be literally a block of land but can be sex, or time of day, in fact anything where a complete mini-set of observations can be done within one set of circumstances and then compared with another complete mini-set done in a different set of circumstances. For example, observations on the male/female differences in behaviour we discussed earlier might inevitably have to be carried out at different times of day or even on different days, so you could 'block' by time of day (or day), provided you had carried out both male and female observations in each 'block' of time.

If you adopted a design such as the one shown in Fig. 4.3, you would end up with information about both differences in behaviour between the sexes (the statistical equivalent of varieties of barley) and about the effects of different times of observations (the equivalent of position in a field). Note that the designs suggested in Fig. 4.3 are not truly *randomized* block designs, but use various forms of balancing within a block.

In this example, the blocks might be different days of observation or they might be observations you do in different locations. Perhaps, if you observed in different places on different days, the blocks would be a combination of day and location so that you would not know which factor contributed most to the differences between blocks. As long as you were primarily concerned with the differences between males and females, this would not matter and you would simply lump day and location into one conglomerate 'between-block' variance.

Blocking or matching is particularly useful for observational studies where your study animals are very heterogeneous and you are faced with a large amount of variation that could otherwise potentially make it difficult to draw valid conclusions. For example, suppose you were testing the hypothesis that single lambs tend to stay closer to their mothers than twin lambs, but the only lambs you could find were all of different ages. This could be a problem because older lambs might be found further from their mothers anyway, so you would have to ensure that you were not inadvertently looking at younger single lambs and older twin lambs. The next best thing to having lambs all of the same age is to do the study on lambs of mixed ages and block them by lamb age. This would mean choosing one singleton lamb and one of two twin lambs of the same age, and comparing their behaviour as one block or matched set of observations, with the prediction that the singleton would be closer to its mother than either of the twins. Then you could repeat the observations with other singleton/twin blocks of the same age, making the same comparison each time. It would not matter that some of your matched sets (blocks) were older or younger than other sets, because in each case you would be making your comparisons between lambs of the same age. If, regardless of age, each comparison showed that the twin lamb was consistently further away from the ewe than the single lamb, you could really believe the result because it is consistent across ages. By blocking or matching for age, you can distinguish the same age variation between singletons and twins, which is what you are really interested in, from the unwanted variation due to the age of the lambs. You have made it more likely that your results on singleton/twins will be significant because you have removed—by the design of your observations—the confounding effects of lamb age.

4.3.1 Matching animals with themselves

Because individual animals can vary so much in their behaviour, a very powerful use for this blocking approach is matching each animal with *itself* under two or more different conditions. For example, if you want to know whether animals are more active in the morning than in the evening, and you suspect that some individuals are just bolder and more active anyway, a good way of dealing with this is to compare each animal's activity in the morning with the same animal's activity in the afternoon. That way, the bolder animals will be even more active in the morning than they are in the afternoon and the less active ones will be only slightly more active. They could be a lot less active overall but still show a distinct morning/afternoon difference, and it is that difference that you are interested in. Blocking by individual (that is, matching each animal with itself) will enable you to separate the effects of time of day (which you are interested in) from those of individual variation or other factors you are not particularly interested in.

Matching an individual with itself does not have to stop at just observing it twice. It can usefully be extended to multiple observations, for example, in studying how behaviour develops over time. Counting the number of times/hour a lamb suckles from its mother when it is newly born, and then making repeated observations at weekly intervals on the same lamb's behaviour, would be a good way of showing how lamb behaviour changes with age. Then, if you did the same set of repeated observations for many independent lambs, each growing up and changing in the same way, you would have a clear picture of developmental changes in lamb suckling behaviour. You would have independent differences between lambs (which might be quite marked because of breed, personality of ewe etc), but these would not obscure the within lamb changes that were also occurring as each lamb grew up.

I have had students gaze at me in horror when I have suggested such a design for their projects. Having thoroughly (and quite correctly) taken on board the importance of independent observations (Principle 1), they concluded that the one thing they must never do is to use more than one observation from each animal. The idea of setting out to test or observe one animal repeatedly clearly strikes them as positively immoral. It is therefore very important to be quite clear why making repeated observations on the same animal under the same conditions (which certainly does violate the requirement for independence) is quite different from matching animals with themselves under two or more different conditions. The first is a statistically invalid way of inflating your sample size. The second is a statistically valid way of reducing unexplained background variance.

4.4   Pseudo-replication or matching?

We have already discussed the dangers of pseudo-replication (section 4.1). If you make repeated observations on the same animal, those observations are highly likely to be more similar (less independent) than if they were made on different animals. So where one animal is matched with itself, for example, it is observed in the morning and again in the evening, or at different ages, wouldn't this be pseudo-replication? Isn't this the very thing that Principle 1 tells us to avoid?

Not necessarily. Matching is not pseudo-replication. If we expect to get the same result because we observe the same animal more than once, then this would indeed be pseudo-replication. But if we expect to get a *different* result (such as that an animal will behave differently depending whether it is out in the open or close to cover), and the same is true of all the other animals we look at, this is actually quite surprising. We are getting consistent differences *despite* the fact that we are watching exactly the same individuals. If the *same* animals consistently *change* their behaviour depending on time of day, this is a particularly powerful piece of evidence that time of day matters.

If in doubt about whether you are wrongly using non-independent data (Principle 1) or correctly reducing error variance by matching (Principle 3), ask yourself the following question. Are you predicting that the animal should behave in the same way on two or more occasions (or more like itself than like any other animal) because it is the same animal, or are you predicting that it will behave differently despite the fact that it is the same animal? If the hypothesis you are testing predicts that the same animal should do the same behaviour on different occasions, that suggests there is a clear danger of pseudo-replication and you should avoid this for the reasons we have already discussed. But if your hypothesis is that the same animal should show different behaviour on different occasions, then you are probably in the clear and set to employ a powerful blocking design by matching each animal with itself under different conditions. But the very fact that this distinction is a difficult one to make illustrates once again the message from Chapter 2—the crucial importance of being clear about exactly what question you are asking. Your question determines not only what kind of evidence you need to collect in general, but it will also follow you right down to the details of your programme of research, and determine whether you can or cannot use observations from the same animal.

4.5   The three principles in practice

There is not just one right way of observing behaviour any more than there is just one right way of designing an experiment. The three principles of good design are useful guides, but they will result in very different programmes of observation, depending on what particular hypothesis you are testing. And essential though they are to the success of any project, they are not in themselves enough to tell you what to actually do when you observe animal behaviour. What we have to do next is to show how the principles can be applied to your particular hypothesis. We are now about to move on from general principles to the collection of specific data.

1) The principles of good experimental design are equally important for good observational design.
2) Replication must be independent (Principle 1).
3) Variables must not be confounded (Principle 2).
4) Unwanted variation must be removed (Principle 3).
5) Matched or blocked observations, in which the behaviour of an animal is matched with itself, is a powerful tool in animal behaviour and should not be confused with pseudo-replication.

5 The selective observer

A big temptation when you start any study of behaviour is to try to record absolutely everything that an animal is doing, 'just in case' it comes in useful at some later stage. This is, however, impossible to achieve in practice and not even particularly desirable. Even a small group of animals can appear confusingly busy and is capable of generating an enormous amount of data in a very short time. To capture everything about their behaviour, you would have to record not only what one animal is doing in terms of how it moves its head, body, and limbs but what all the other animals around it are doing as well and how the behaviour of all of them changes from moment to moment. You would have to record where all the animals are in relation to both other animals and features of their environment and which animals are interacting with which others. You would need to record the sounds they are all making and, for some species, their colour patterns and displays. You would be very quickly overwhelmed by data. If only for the sake of your own sanity, you have, therefore, to be very selective in what you choose to record. In this chapter, we will look at how to be selective in what you observe and still get what you want out of your data.

5.1 Levels of observation

You first have to decide the level (group–individual–body part) you are going to study. To see what 'level' means, suppose you had decided to test a hypothesis that predicted that animals should be found in larger groups the further away they are from the cover of trees. To test this, you would need to record the size of the groups you were observing, but you might not need to record the behaviour of each individual animal. This particular prediction would be upheld or rejected depending on what the whole group does, so you need a group level measure, such as group size, to test it. On the other hand, if you had predicted that animals should look up more and feed less the further away from cover they were, you would need to observe at the level of the individual and record some measure of what individuals did, such as the number of times they raised their heads per minute. In neither of these cases would you necessarily have to count the number of steps or leg movements an animal took, whereas if you were studying sheep in a field and you had predicted that they would feed more and walk less when they encountered certain sorts of plants, the number of steps an individual took would be very relevant to this particular prediction (body part level description).

So there is no simple right or wrong way of recording behaviour—just ways that are appropriate or inappropriate to the testing of your particular hypothesis. That simple question from Tinbergen, 'What question are you asking?', has cropped up yet again, this time mercifully letting you off the hook of having to record everything that every animal is doing. The question gives you permission to be selective in what you record and actually makes it easier, not more difficult, to provide convincing tests of your hypotheses.

Don't worry about having to be selective. All biological measurements are to some extent selective because no-one can measure everything. This chapter and the next one are about how to be appropriately selective in what you observe about animal behaviour. 'Appropriate' here means selecting the appropriate time scale (where the choice is from seconds to weeks or years), the appropriate level (where the choice is from an individual's whisker twitch to mass migrations of whole herds), and the appropriate sampling regime (what, for how long, and how often you record). In Chapter 6 we will look at some basic ways of sampling behaviour and see that they can be easily adapted to different sorts of questions, such as when the behaviour occurs, where it happens, and the kinds of social interactions that might be going on.

But we have already got ahead of ourselves. We cannot decide what the appropriate time scale, level, or sampling regime should be until we have tackled some much more fundamental questions about behaviour itself. What *is* behaviour? What do animals actually do? How do we choose what to record?

5.2   Selecting units: what is 'behaviour'?

At first sight, behaviour appears to have no building blocks, no equivalent of the cells or organs that build up a physical body. Nor does it appear to have units that can be measured like units of heat or light or length. It appears to be ephemeral, elusive, and constantly shifting, a will-o'-the wisp that defies definition. But if you look for a while longer, you will see that not only does it have units of its own, those units can also be measured and quantified.

The key to recognizing units of behaviour is that animals do not behave at random. Animals could, from the way their muscles are put together, move their heads and bodies in all sorts of ways, but they only move them in a restricted sub-set of ways. They could produce movements in all sorts of sequences with limbs flailing all over the place, swallowing before they chew, or trying to build the sides of a nest before they have laid the foundations. But they don't. The movements they produce are highly coordinated in both time and space. Their sequences of movement are the opposite of random. They are highly patterned.

These patterned sequences of movement are the fundamental units of behaviour and they can be measured just as surely as we can measure an animal's weight or the number of bristles on its tail. Most people recognize behaviour patterns and define the units they are going to measure by using the 'computer in the head' (their own brain), which is extraordinarily good at detecting repeated patterns on a time scale of a few seconds. Usually it is not too difficult for even a complete novice to pick out identifiable behaviour patterns such as 'pecking', 'scratching' or 'foot-paddling' as repeated sequences of movement taking a few seconds to complete.

The fact that different observers can agree on what these behaviour patterns are suggests that this method is not nearly as arbitrary as it might sound. The patterns of behaviour do seem to be genuinely there because the computers in different heads are picking up the same units. You know exactly what I mean by 'pecking' or 'flying' because your brain will have picked out these common and highly distinctive behaviour patterns itself. You may need a bit more explanation of what is meant by some of the more unusual behaviours such as 'foot-paddling' in gulls or—my own favourite—'post-copulatory steaming' in ducks (McKinney, 1965). But, armed with a description of what these behaviours look like, you too would be able to recognize them, for the simple reason that gulls and ducks in the future will produce non-random sequences of movement that are very similar to the sequences observed and described by other people in the past.

The complete list of all the behaviour patterns an animal has in its repertoire is called its *ethogram*, and a good way to start a study of any species is to spend some time watching what it does and writing down a list of what you see it doing. A period of apparently unstructured observation can be very helpful for your more systematic data collection later on because you will effectively be training the computer in your head by 'just watching'. You will notice the repeated movement patterns and be able to use these as the basis of your future recordings. Reading what has been published on this species already may also help but, even if you know what units other people have used, it is still worth constructing your own list or ethogram. You might find that the units other people have used were inconvenient, inaccurate, or simply not appropriate for your hypothesis. Someone else might have identified 'sitting' but made no distinction between 'sitting with eyes open' and 'sitting with eyes closed' because they were only interested in whether the animals were sitting down or standing up. You, on the other hand, might be testing a quite different hypothesis, such as that having seen a predator within the last hour makes these animals subsequently more likely to keep their eyes open. You would clearly want to record sitting with eyes open and sitting with eyes closed as two quite separate behaviour patterns.

And it may not just be the behaviour of individual animals that you want to observe. Whole *groups* of animals behave too. Flocks of starlings wheel through the sky in fantastic spirals, schools of fish move together (Fig. 5.1), and ant colonies form orderly two-way highways to and from a food source (Dussutour et al., 2005). You may be interested in testing hypotheses about how the whole group is behaving rather than attempting to record what every individual is doing, or you may want to do both. A thriving area of behaviour is the study of collective behaviour—how the behaviour of flocks and herds can be understood from the behaviour of its component individuals (Couzin and Krause, 2003), so that both a group and an individual description may be needed for the same study.

Going the other way, we can observe behaviour at a level below that of an individual animal, and ask how *individual body parts* such as wings or feet contribute to the movement of the whole body. A description of foot-paddling, for example, might include a detailed analysis—perhaps using frame by frame video—of exactly how gulls move their feet. Some hypotheses about foot-paddling, such as those about the effect the gulls have on the properties of mud, might need accurate measurements of how fast the gulls are moving their feet and how they move them; whereas other hypotheses, such as those about the effects of tides or weather, could be tested without any such detailed measurements at all.

Fig. 5.1   The behaviour of animals, such as these blackbar soldierfish, can be studied as a whole group or as individuals. © Oxford University Press.

Although it may not seem like it yet, you have already come a long way from that imaginary moment on the harbour wall. Then, your mind was not initially focused on animal behaviour until something odd happened and you were forced to take notice and start wondering what was going on. That wondering has been through the discipline of having to ask a specific question and formulate a specific hypothesis. Now it is being further disciplined by focusing again on the behaviour and asking exactly what the animal is doing. You have to do the equivalent of going back to the harbour and watching the gulls again. This time, your watching is far from idle and you have to concentrate on describing exactly what they are doing. What behaviour patterns can you identify? What are the units of behaviour that you might use to test your hypothesis?

The longer and more closely you watch, however, the longer and more complicated your list of behaviours is likely to become. Animals such as gulls have very complex behavioural repertoires and there may be a lot going on at any one time. One gull may attempt to steal something another has just found. A dog in the distance may cause the whole group to keep looking up. And there is not just one gull but many, some doing the same things, some doing different things, so that the idea of trying to record all the behaviour you can identify seems increasingly difficult. Too much is happening all at once. That is where a second type of selection has to start operating. You may have described your units of behaviour from amongst all the possible movements your animals could make, but you now have to select among those units so that you record the ones that are most relevant to testing your particular hypothesis.

5.3   Selecting behaviour patterns

You cannot record every behaviour pattern an animal has in its ethogram. Even if you make video records, you still have to watch the videos or analyse them with some hypothesis in mind. Very large databases derived from the results of automatic recording devices may give the illusion of telling you all you ever wanted to know about behaviour, but they still have to be interrogated in a hypothesis-based way. They can't give you 'all the answers' about behaviour. They can only give you specific answers to specific questions, so you still have to be selective. At some stage in every behavioural project, you have to face up to the disappointing fact that you will 'miss' some behaviour. This is, in fact, a blessing in disguise, because just having vast amounts of data does not guarantee the success of any research project. As we have repeatedly seen, science is not about accumulating facts. The best science is about selectively collecting facts that test predictions from hypotheses. By being selective in what behaviour you record, therefore, you may well find it easier to do better science because you are forced at an early stage in your investigation to focus on what you need to test your hypothesis. The mountains of data you could have collected had you had the time and equipment could actually be a distraction from this central process of hypothesis testing. So be strong minded and focus on the key question: 'What data do I need to test the hypothesis that . . . ?'.

For example, if you are testing a hypothesis that predicts that a particular species of animal is more likely to sit down in cool weather than in hotter weather, then it is clearly essential to record both sitting and it's opposite, standing up. But it is not vital to the test of this hypothesis that you record how much the animal grooms itself or plays with other animals. Although these behaviours are interesting in their own right and might, conceivably, be relevant to why temperature has this effect on behaviour, they are at this stage optional extras— things it might be nice to record but not essential. And if they distract you from the test of your main hypothesis and make it difficult to record the data you do need, they are a positive nuisance and should be avoided.

Your selected list of behaviours to record thus has to include first and foremost behaviour that is essential to the test of your main hypothesis, but even this will be too much. Even your pruned-down, slim-line list of behaviours would present you with insurmountable practical problems if you attempted to record every time any of your animals did any of them, night or day, for as long as your study lasted. You would have no time for eating or sleeping. You wouldn't be able to take your eyes of any of them for a minute and you might be frantically trying to watch several animals at once. You therefore have to be selective not only in *what* behaviour you record from each animal but also in *how long you spend observing* it. In other words, what you record and the actual time you spend observing behaviour is a small *sample* of what you might ideally like to record. Film, video, and other types of automated recording will help to increase what you can record, but they will still only give you small samples of an animals' total behaviour, and you still have to decide whether to use the whole of every record or just small sections. The right sampling regime is as important for automated observation as is it for actual observation. The only difference is at what stage you are forced to be selective. If you know you are going to get cold and wet from sitting outside, you will tend to take a decision about how long and how often to watch at an earlier stage in your study than if you can delay such decisions until the moment you sit down to analyse a pile of videotapes. But they will have to be taken at some stage.

5.4 Selecting samples of behaviour

Taking a series of small samples to give a representative picture of the whole is a well established necessity in biology. In fact, the whole field of statistics can be thought of as the science of arriving at valid conclusions when the measurements available are only a small fraction of everything you could possibly have measured. The trick is to make sure that the samples you take are truly representative of all the animals you might measure. We are now going to look at how to take representative samples of behaviour.

5.4.1   Scan sampling

If you are watching a large group of animals, you may not be able to watch all of them all of the time, but you may be able to watch all of them for some of the time. An easy way of doing this is to do a quick scan of the whole group and count the numbers with, say, their heads up and the numbers feeding. This would give you a 'snapshot' of what they were all doing at one moment in time. Some time later, you could do another scan and capture another frozen moment in time. This method of recording behaviour is known as *scan sampling* and is obviously easiest and quickest to do if you are scanning for something simple such as numbers with heads up. It becomes more difficult (and therefore less instantaneous) the more behaviours you try to record each time you make a scan.

Scan sampling is particularly suitable for testing hypotheses about the behaviour of whole groups of animals, because you ignore many of the details of the behaviour of individuals but gain information about what everybody is doing at once. Remember that although you may be watching a group of, say, 30 animals, you do not have 30 independent samples, because 30 animals in one group are not independent of each other as we discussed in Chapter 4 (Principle 1). So even if all 30 of the birds had their heads raised, you can only count it as one flock, one independent replicate. You need to find many more separate flocks to scan in order to increase your sample size.

5.4.2   Focal animal sampling

A useful alternative to scan sampling a whole group is to concentrate on just one individual animal and use what is called *focal animal sampling*—recording everything that one animal does over a set period of time, such as 10 or 20 minutes. No notice is taken of what any other animals in the group are doing, except in so far as what they do impinges on the focal animal, for example, if they bite it, or bump into it, or are bitten or bumped into by it. At the end of the observation period some summary statistic, such as the mean number of times the focal animal looked up, or how long it suckled from its mother, is extracted from the record and becomes one data point in a whole series of your observations. Because the focal animal is taken as representative of that whole group, this means that you have to be particularly careful in deciding which of a group of animals is chosen to be the focus of your observations.

Consistently choosing the cutest or the most active or the animal that happens to be closest to you could bias the results and even invalidate the whole study. So make sure you watch a randomly chosen animal, as discussed in Chapter 4 (Principle 2, section 4.2.3).

5.4.3   Other kinds of sampling

Both scan sampling and focal animal sampling can be carried out systematically in such a way that you can apply all three principles of good design. By being careful about the time of day at which you take the samples, for example, you can make sure that this does not confound your results. You can deliberately choose independent animals and you can reduce background variation by blocking your observations. But sometimes your well designed protocol may be thrown to the wind by the animals themselves. Wild animals go about their lives in their own way (and this is what makes them so interesting) but that means that they will often not conform to a carefully designed schedule of systematic sampling. They may not be around when your next scan or focal observation sample is due to take place. They violate all criteria for independence by interacting socially or visiting each other's territories. They refuse, unlike the crop plants for which statistical methods were originally designed, to stay in their designated plots or blocks. My carefully designed proposal for observing wild Red Junglefowl at hourly intervals throughout the day in the forests of Thailand, for example, (a design that worked perfectly well on a feral population in England) had to be completely abandoned when I got to Thailand and realized that I would be lucky to catch a glimpse of these extremely shy birds even once a day at dawn.

There will be many occasions, in other words, when you simply do not have the ability to make the systematic observations you would ideally like to have, or to incorporate all the possible features of good design. So what can you do? If you are studying a little known species and you see it doing a rare behaviour, you would be crazy not to record what it was doing just because it wasn't part of your sampling schedule at that moment. Or if you caught sight of an extremely secretive animal that was so rarely seen in the wild that no-one knew very much about its behaviour at all, then it could be very important to record everything it was doing as that might be your only chance to get any data at all.

These two situations are referred to as '*behaviour sampling*' (if you see the behaviour at all, record it) and *ad libitum sampling* (if you see the animal at all, record anything it is doing) respectively (Altmann, 1974). Both methods are particularly suitable for rare events or ones that are unpredictable, such as exactly when one stag is going to challenge another or when a female is going to approach a male. In both such cases, it is best to seize the moment and record everything that you see. Your observations can then be put together to form set of case notes, which can subsequently be sorted into categories such as encounters between two large stags, those between one large and one small stag etc. You can also see whether your observations refer to different individuals, or always the same ones, and so get an idea retrospectively of how many independent individuals you are dealing with. You may then set out to collect information on the 'missing' individuals or categories, and so increase the validity of the whole set.

Such observations, taken together, can yield very valuable information, but because they are not taken systematically, they may give you a somewhat unrepresentative picture of the animals' behaviour as a whole. They are therefore unsuitable for questions such as those involving the amount of time an animal spends doing a behaviour during the day, because you may only be able to see it at one time of day. You are also most likely to record the behaviour of the most conspicuous animals or the ones that are least afraid of humans, and so are in danger of getting an atypical picture of the behaviour of that species.

If you do find yourself in a situation where behaviour sampling or *ad libitum* sampling are the only options open to you, and/or you have only one group of a rare animal to study, the best strategy is to pick a question that you can answer using these approaches rather than attempting to answer one for which you will only be able to gather poor quality data. For example, if your animals are difficult to find and you can only ever get glimpses of them for half an hour at a time, don't ask a question about how behaviour varies with time of day or how animals allocate their time to different activities because it is going to be impossible for you to collect the data you need. Nobody is going to be convinced that you have tested a hypothesis about sex differences in behaviour on the basis of your having seen two males for twenty minutes each and one female for forty minutes. And they won't accept it as an excuse that you had to go to great lengths and climb a treacherous cliff face and sit out in the sun for several hours to get even that data.

What you can do, however, is to ask questions that you can hope to answer with erratic, opportunistic observations. Hrdy's (1974) observations on langurs showed that infanticide by males was not, as everyone had believed, a rare pathological event, but a common occurrence whenever a new male took over a group. She obviously could not predict when infanticide was going to occur. She just had to record the events that took place when a new male moved in. By observing these relatively rare events whenever she could, Hrdy was able to establish that killing of infants happened almost every time and, indeed, was an adaptive feature of male behaviour.

The choice of what sort of sampling (scan, focal animal, behaviour, and *ad libitum*) to use thus depends on two factors. One is simply what is available to you. The other is what your exact question is. Each one affects the other and compromises may have to be reached. If you are tempted to ask a question that can only be answered with data that you know are going to be impossible to collect, or that are very difficult to locate, then *don't ask that question*. Ask another question that you can hope to answer. But before we get onto what these are, there is yet another kind of selection we have to go through to make a sampling of all kinds easier to use in practice.

5.5   Selecting the type of measurement

Even when you have decided to observe behaviour over a short sample of time, you still have a choice over how much of what you observe you actually record. A *continuous* record of behaviour includes not just every behaviour an animal does, but the exact times it starts and stops each time. If the animal behaves relatively slowly, as cattle tend to, you will probably be able to keep up, even with direct observation, by glancing at your watch and noting the times of any change in behaviour. But if the animal keeps changing behaviour rapidly, you may not be able to keep up or, worse, you may lose track of it in the effort to write everything down.

Continuous recording with precise information about when behaviour stops and starts gives you very good quality data, known as *interval measurements* (Siegel and Castellan, 1988), which can be used for all sorts of statistical analyses (section 8.4). There are many occasions, however, when a continuous record is not, in fact, absolutely necessary to a project, and it may be possible to test a hypothesis just as effectively by recording less about each behaviour. This makes it much easier to write down what you observe (or record from a video) and allows you to keep up with the animal's behaviour in real time. It might be enough to record just whether or not the behaviour occurred *at all* during the sampling period. You could use what is known as *zero/one (yes-no) sampling*, which greatly simplifies the recording process.

What this means is that you watch your focal animal for the same amount of time as for continuous sampling, but you only write down whether or not it did a behaviour. Did it or did it not go to the salt lick? Did it or did it not suckle from its mother? This gives you what is known as *categorical measurements* (Siegel and Castellan, 1988), which are perfectly valid but can only be used in certain types of statistical test (section 8.4.2). Categorical measurements are extremely useful when we are looking for clear cut differences between different outcomes or categories, such as the number of adult males vocalizing versus the number of juvenile males vocalizing. They are also very useful when looking at animal choices, when the numbers of animals choosing option A versus the numbers choosing option B gives a clear indication as to whether there is a preference for A over B.

A compromise between the comprehensiveness of interval measurements and the sparseness of categorical measurements is a third category of measurement that is very commonly used in behavioural research and that you may well want to use yourself. This is *ordered or ranked measurements* (Siegel and Castellan, 1988), which can be very useful wherever it is possible to say that an animal does more of something than another, but not possible to say exactly how much more. For example, you might be able to say that one animal is more aggressive than others and you could rank or order the animals on an 'aggressiveness' scale (measured, say, by the number of attacks they initiated), but you could not measure points on that scale precisely or say that being 'highly aggressive' always meant showing the same combination of behaviours. Some highly aggressive males might slash with their horns while others might kick or use their teeth. Some would do no more than push their opponent with their shoulders, but sometimes the shoulderpushing would become so violent that the other male would reel and fall over.

With such very variable behaviour all contributing to 'aggression', it can be a good solution to devise a rank or ordered measurement of the behaviour. Instead of trying to record all the individual behaviour patterns, you could simply divide the behaviour into categories. These might be: 1 = approach to within 15 metres; 2 = approach to within 2 metres but with no physical encounter; 3 = mild physical touching with no injury or pushing; 4 = pushing but no injury; and 5 = physical encounter leading to injury. Provided your definitions are clear and other people can see exactly what you mean, this can be a very pragmatic way of measuring the behaviour, one that enables you to rank animals as more or less aggressive than others. Ordered or rank measurements have to be analysed with non-parametric statistical tests (section 8.5), but as these are very easy to carry out and make few assumptions about the data, this is no great handicap. On the contrary, the ease of making ordered or rank measurements, and the number of different sorts of data that can be treated in this way, makes them an important part of behavioural research.

You may be concerned about the accuracy or reliability of incomplete records such as zero/one measures, or the somewhat arbitrary categories that go into ranked measurements. Of course it is better to be more accurate than less accurate, but accuracy comes with a cost. It may be difficult or impossible to obtain complete records with an accurate time base, or you may miss vital events if you try to record everything. The important thing to be sure about is that any loss of accuracy does not *confound* your results (Chapter 4, Principle 2). As long as the type of measurement is no more likely to produce inaccurate or arbitrary results for, say, males than females, then there is no problem with confounding sex with measurement type. As long as you are consistent in how you make the measurements, the loss of accuracy or arbitrariness will affect observations on both males and females equally. All the observations may be less accurate as a result of your choosing zero/one rather than continuous recording, but the most that is likely to happen is that you will make it more difficult to detect any difference between the two sexes. This means that if you do find a difference, you can confidently rely on it. There must have been such a large difference between the sexes that it showed up despite your 'approximate' method of recording.

5.6 What is 'appropriate' selection of behaviour?

Throughout all this discussion of being selective in what you observe has been the assumption that the 'appropriate' way of choosing everything, from what units to record, to how long to spend watching and how much detail to record, was completely dependent on the particular project you were engaged in. I have tried to give an idea of the range of possibilities, but this may have left you a bit bewildered as to exactly what you should do for your own particular project. It is now time to see how different types of question lead you to make different choices and select rather different ways of actually recording behaviour. I have deliberately included some actual examples so that you can see how observational studies work in practice.

Most hypotheses about animal behaviour lead us to ask questions that fall into one of six (overlapping) categories: *What? How much? Where? When? Who?* and *With whom? What?* questions, as we have seen, form the basis for all others (section 5.2). You need to know what your animals are doing before you can ask anything else. Sometimes *What?* questions are sufficient in themselves, perhaps because nobody has ever seen the behaviour before or at least not seen it in that level of detail (Chapter 3), so a description in itself would justify publication. Most studies, on the other hand, combine *What?* questions with one or more of the other five. This is because most hypotheses about animal behaviour make predictions about *amount* of behaviour (such as that males will be more aggressive than females), *timing* (behaviour will regularly occur at dawn or after something else has happened), *place* (animals will be found where there is a concentration of minerals), *individual identity* (different animals consistently behave differently), or *association* (animals will have particular mutual grooming partners). These predictions now need to be matched to the 'appropriate' type of behaviour sampling you need to do for your project. We start with the most basic kind of behavioural measurements, the building blocks for other sorts of measurements.

5.7 How much? Measuring the 'amount' of behaviour

One of the kinds of prediction you are most likely to make from any behavioural hypothesis will involve you having to measure *how much* behaviour animals are doing. For example, if you had predicted that animals on the edge of a group should be more vigilant than those in the centre, you would be in the business of measuring the amount of vigilant behaviour going on. To do this, you could measure:

- The *duration* of the behaviour (how long the animal spends looking around).
- The *frequency* with which it does it (how many times it looks around within a certain time).
- The *intensity* with which it does it (the strength of its responses; in the case of vigilance one measure might be how high the animals raised their heads).

5.7.1 Measuring 'how much?' using duration

Although each of these is a measure of 'how much' behaviour an animal is doing, they do not necessarily give you the same answer. For example, if we measured 'how much' roaring different individual Red deer stags do by measuring the duration of their roars, the number of roars they give per minute (frequency), and the loudness of their roars (intensity), we might get different answers to the question of which stag did the most roaring. One might be roaring twice as often as the others but roaring very quietly, or one might roar only occasionally but its roars may be longer each time. Sometimes it is important to employ more than one measure, for example, where you don't know what another animal is responding to and where an important part of the study would be to find out. At other times, you may adopt one or another, depending on the precise nature of your predictions and the practicalities of the situation.

To record the duration of behaviour you obviously need a way of measuring the amount of time the animal spends doing it. This can be done either as the proportion of the time you spent observing the animal that it spent doing behaviour A (e.g. the animal spent 5 out of the 10 minutes (50%) sitting down). Or you could break the total duration down into its constituent bouts (e.g. out of the 10 minute observation period, the animal sat down twice, once for 2 minutes and 4 seconds, and once for 2 minutes. 56 seconds). It is often worth analysing the behaviour in both ways because they may give different answers. For example, the total amount of time a rabbit spends looking around could be taken as one measure of its 'vigilance' and would be the sum of all the looking around times when it has repeatedly looked up, bent down to feed, and looked up again. On the other hand, it may be that the durations of each individual time the rabbit looks up has significance. Perhaps you are testing a hypothesis that in some kinds of environment the rabbit should look up little and often, and in other kinds of environment it should look up less often but for more time. The total duration of vigilance might be the same but the individual bout lengths might be different.

Video records are an easy way of obtaining information about the durations of behaviour but a notebook and stopwatch will often serve remarkably well too. The convenience and simplicity of writing down the durations of behaviour directly often pay off if you are concentrating on just a single behaviour such as the duration of successive dives made by a cormorant. And you don't have to worry about the video camera getting wet in the boat, either.

5.7.2 Measuring 'how much?' by frequency

There is some behaviour, however, that takes place so rapidly that, at least to the naked eye, it has no measurable duration at all. A single peck of a chick or a single step of a shore bird is best classified as an act or event, effectively a point in time with no duration. Of course, if you were to record the behaviour on film or video and then slow it down, it would obviously have a measurable duration, but to the naked eye it looks instantaneous. Where behaviour takes place so rapidly that you hardly have time to note the time it starts before the behaviour has already stopped, it is best to regard the behaviour as a point act with no duration and to measure the *frequency* with which it occurs. For example, if you make a small mark (or press a tally counter or key on a keyboard) every time you see an animal pecking and note the total time you spend watching it, you will end up with a very useful quantitative measure of how much pecking it has done: the frequency or the number of pecks the animal does per unit time. If the behaviour takes place so rapidly that even this is impossible, it may be best to treat the whole *bout* (repeated sequence the same behaviour) as the unit, with a duration of its own. For example, if a thrush or blackbird (*Turdus*) runs rapidly and then stops, and then runs again and stops, it may be impossible to record the *frequency* of its steps and much more feasible to record the *duration* of its bouts of *running*

5.7.3 Measuring 'bouts' of behaviour

The choice of whether to record frequency of individual units or duration of bouts of those units is not, however, entirely a matter of convenience. There are sound statistical reasons for not pushing yourself to record every little detail, particularly where the same behaviour is repeated in rapid succession.

The issue of non-independence (Principle 1, Chapter 4) raises its head again here, this time urging us to record less not more.

Why has the shadow of non-independence arisen again here? After all, we are sitting out in the sunshine, recording behaviour of one animal, admittedly, but with every intention of moving on and finding other independent animals or groups on which to make the rest of our observations. The sky appears to be completely blue. Where could any non-independence be coming from? Oddly enough, it is coming from the animals themselves and from the very fact that they repeat their behaviour.

Pecking is a good example of behaviour with non-independence almost built into the way it is performed. Domestic chicks rarely peck just once at objects they cannot immediately eat. If an object turns out to be inedible, the chick almost always pecks it several times in a row. A barrage of six-pecks bouts, all delivered in rapid succession to the same object, are not independent of each other in just the same way that six seconds or six minutes or six hours of lying down in cattle are not. If a chick always pecks in bouts of six, then we might be on safer ground statistically to count the bouts of six pecks as 'one bout of pecking' and measure the duration of the bout rather than six independent instances and measure frequency. In other words, there is so much pattern or predictability in the behaviour that the sequence of six pecks has become a 'behaviour pattern' in its own right and should be considered as a single unit (section 5.2).

Of course, real chicks do not always give exactly six pecks in a row so the question would arise: how predictable does a sequence of repeated behaviour have to be before we have to count it as a bout or unit in its own right? Don't be alarmed by the fact that this turns out to be an extremely complex question (Berdoy, 1993; Langton et al., 1995; Tolkamp and Kyriazakos, 1999) and that many papers have been written not only on the exact definition of a bout, but on how to judge when behaviour patterns become independent of one another. Rest assured that many researchers in animal behaviour get by without worrying about this issue too much at all. By even being aware of it and thinking about whether you should be recording durations of bouts or frequency of individual acts, you are one jump ahead of many people. A good rule of thumb is that if your animal is so predictable that once it starts doing something you know exactly what it is going to do next (another five pecks say, or stretching its left leg when it has just stretched its right), lump everything together as one bout of pecking or one bout of stretching. But if, as is much more likely, your animal is somewhat unpredictable, you may need to set up some definitions of your own, such as a walking bout is when the animal walks continuously without stopping, and the end of the bout is defined when it stops for at least five seconds. As long as you are clear about this when you report on what you have done, that's fine.

5.7.4 Measuring 'how much?' by intensity

The third way of measuring the 'amount' of behaviour is by its *intensity*. This can mean measuring, say, the loudness of a sound an animal is making, in which case the resulting data are interval measurements (section 5.5) measured in physical units such as decibels. Such data can be analysed using ordinary parametric statistical tests (Chapter 8). But intensity can also mean a high score on an ordered or rank scale that cannot be directly related to physical units. 'Aggressiveness' (section 5.5) would be a good example. An animal can be described as very aggressive or less aggressive on an intensity scale that is defined objectively but not in physical units. The analysis of such data will probably need non-parametric statistical tests (Chapter 8), but rank scales have many uses in the study of behaviour, particularly in field studies where accurate measurements may be difficult to obtain.

Even if there are practical reasons why you cannot catch and weigh animals in the wild, you can still estimate relative body weight or shoulder height and rank them on an intensity score of body weight. You might try to assess shoulder height relative to a mark on a tree, or estimate differences in between the two males by eye, or even just categorize each male as 'small' (=1), medium (=2), or large (=3). Each of these measures would be only a very rough guide to the actual body weight and height of the stags, rather than exact measurements in kilogrammes or centimetres, but they can be useful and they can also be validated. Photographs of what you mean by small, medium, and large stags, plus detailed written criteria will help, and you should check yourself from time to time to make sure that your current categorization of stags hasn't 'slipped' from your original ranking.

In general, intensity scores are extremely useful for observational studies and in a variety of situations:

- Where the physical intensity (such as the loudness of a sound or the brightness of light) can be measured using standard instruments.
- When it is difficult or impractical to describe individual behaviour patterns but possible to describe behaviour in terms of broad categories that can be ranked, such as an animal being more or less aggressive.
- When we don't have access to 'proper' detailed measurements and have to estimate into broad categories, such as being able to say that one animal is heavier than another but not how much. For example, if you were testing the hypothesis that animals behaved differently depending on the size of group they were in, it might be impossible to count every individual in a huge flock of starlings, but you could use an intensity scale of flock size such as 'single animals' (no others within a defined distance), small groups (up to four individuals), medium (five or over), and large (hundreds).

5.8 A check list for selection

You now have some basic ideas about how what observing behaviour involves and why it is essential to be selective. To achieve the selection that is right for your particular project, you have to make the following decisions about what you are going to record (or take from a video record):

1) The *level* or levels at which you will be observing (group–individual animal–body part) (section 5.1).
2) The *units* (behaviour patterns) you will record (section 5.2, 5.3).
3) The type of *sampling* (focal animal, scan, *ad libitum*, behaviour) that you will use (section 5.4).
4) The type of *record* (continuous, zero/one, or something in between) with the consequent type of *measurement* you will be able to extract (categorical, ordered (ranked), or interval).
5) And, if you have decided to measure the *amount* of behaviour, whether to record duration, frequency, or intensity.

The next step is to construct a detailed *protocol* or programme of the research.

6 Down to detail

A *protocol* or research plan is a detailed description of what you are actually going to do. It has to be detailed enough that someone else could read it and see exactly what you were going to record, when, where, and in what order. They should be able to reconstruct exactly what you do, right down to the exact time and place of each of your observational samples. If you couldn't be there for some reason, they should be able to fill in exactly what you would have done. It will form the basis for the description of the 'methods' section of any report you write about your research and it also helps you to see, at a relatively early stage in your planning, whether there are likely to be any problems with the project. We start this chapter with some of the commonest issues that you are likely to encounter as you put together your research plans. We will then look at an example of a simple research design and finally discuss how you can come up with a valid protocol for your particular research aims.

6.1 Sample size

An obvious question that everyone asks when they start to put together their research protocol, is how many animals or groups of animals they are going to need. In other words, having decided on how to record behaviour (concentrating on a focal animal, say), what to record (preening and feeding), and how to record it (zero/one in each minute), you are then faced with the problem of how many different focal animals you need to make those observations on. How many independent statistical replicates do there have to be before you can achieve that magical 'statistical significance'? There is, unfortunately, no simple answer to this question. It all depends on two critical factors: how large an effect you are expecting (such as how much difference there is between males and females) and how much background variation there is anyway (how much males and females differ among themselves). Understanding how these two sorts of variation are related to sample size is the first step in working out how many independent replicates you will need to aim for.

We have repeatedly seen that one of the problems with animal behaviour is how variable it is. Males might feed more than females, but some individual males might feed a lot more or less than other individual males. This means that even if there were an average difference in feeding behaviour between males and females, some individual males might eat less than some individual females. The extent of this overlap between males and females is the first clue as to how large a sample size you are going to need. You would need a much larger sample size to pick up the difference between the sexes if there were a lot of overlap than if there were very clear cut differences between the sexes with no female eating more than any male. (Fig. 6.1). The size of the sex difference is also critical. If males eat more than females but only slightly more, then you will need a larger sample size than if males eat massively more than females.

This is the point where biologists and statisticians can come to an apparent impasse. For a statistician, the solution to the problem of how large a sample size is needed is easy. They need to know the extent of the overlap. In other words, they want to know how variable the males and females are amongst themselves (within group variance), and how much variation in behaviour can be ascribed to the sex of the individuals (between group variance). They can then calculate the required sample size for a given degree of statistical significance, using what is called the *power* of the statistical test, which is the probability of rejecting the null hypothesis when it is in fact false (Appendix 2). The biologists, on the other hand, are unimpressed or positively baffled. How on earth do you know what the overlap is without having already done the observations you are planning to make? That's what you are doing the observations *for* in the first place. If you knew all the things the statisticians wanted to know already, you'd have already done the observations anyway.

It all seems like a Catch 22. You can't do your observations until you have decided on your sample size and you can't decide on your sample size until you have done the observations. The solution is an uneasy compromise in which an estimate (often with an element of guess work) is made of the underlying variation and the true differences between groups (Appendix 2). The estimate should ideally be based on a pilot study (Chapter 7) to make sure that they are realistic. This will give you an idea of whether you are dealing with clear cut, non-overlapping differences requiring only a relatively small sample size, or subtle, overlapping ones that may need larger numbers of animals.

6.1.1 Getting the sample size wrong

A sample size that is too large will cost you in time, money, and effort. It will also violate one of the '3Rs' (section 1.7) which are becoming one of the guiding

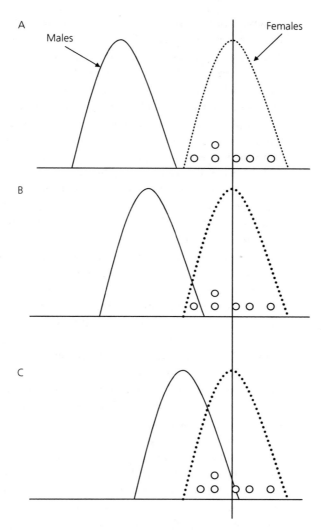

Fig. 6.1 Illustration of how the degree of overlap between two groups affects the chance of picking up that difference with a small sample. The curves represent the true population measurements (in other words, the measurements you would get if you really were able to observe all the males and all the females in the world). The circles represent the observational samples that might actually be made on six females. The corresponding observational samples on males are omitted for clarity. In 'A', males and females are entirely distinct so that none of the observational samples on females are in any danger of being confused with male ones. In 'B', some males resemble females so that one of the female measurements actually looks very like a male, and in 'C', male and female samples will look even more similar. In all three cases there is a real difference between the sexes so that females are, on average, scoring higher than males, but a larger sample size will be needed to pick up a 'significant' difference in 'C' than in 'A'.

principles of all research on animals (www.nc3rs.org.uk). While observational research raises, on the whole, fewer ethical issues than performing experiments on animals, it is still important to consider the possible impact that your study might have on their welfare. The Association for the Study of Animal Behaviour and the Animal Behaviour Society (ASAB/ABS, 2006) have jointly drawn up guidelines for research in animal behaviour which are very helpful. Reduction, replacement and refinement are still important in planning an observational study. Consider the first of the 3 Rs: reduction. Choosing too large a sample size could mean that you have not fully considered the possibility of reducing the total amount of stress your study might cause by reducing the number of animals in the study. That is why doing a proper power calculation, despite the estimations that are inevitably involved, is an important part of your planning. You also don't want to do more work yourself than you absolutely have to.

However, reducing your sample size to a bare minimum is not always ethically desirable, for two reasons. Firstly, animals may be stressed by being separated from one another. Moving individual sheep from their flock into a field where you could observe them on their own might reduce the total number of animals you observed, but they would be highly stressed at being separated from the rest of their flock and their behaviour is likely to be very abnormal. You would be better off, both ethically and in terms of the results you would obtain, by observing more sheep rather than fewer, even if it meant including many flocks in your study. Reduction in this case would conflict directly with the third of the 3 Rs, refinement or improving the welfare impact of what you do.

Secondly, reducing your sample size to the minimum may also be undesirable if it produces that most infuriating of all possible outcomes—the 'nearly' significant result. Of course, there is in reality no such thing as a nearly significant result. Your results will either reach the level of significance you have already decided on before you do the statistical test (Chapter 8) or they will not. But to have set a significance level of, say 0.05 and then to have your results come out as $p = 0.06$, with almost all the animals behaving in the way predicted by your hypothesis, but not quite enough of them, leaves you, strictly speaking, with only one option. You (or somebody else at a later stage) will have to repeat the whole set of observations with a larger sample size. The result is more work, more expense, and more animals involved than if you had used a larger sample size in the first place. So, even from an ethical point of view, reduction does not necessarily mean reducing numbers as far as you possibly can. A larger sample size can, through giving a better result, ultimately result in the use of fewer animals.

6.2   Sample length and sample interval

The length of time you observe and how often you observe will also depend on the particular behaviour you are watching. Ten minutes once an hour might be adequate if you were studying behaviour such as roosting or grazing, because these behaviours continue for a sufficiently long time that you would be likely to see them. But if you were studying a behaviour that is either very infrequent and/or takes only a few seconds to do, then you might well miss the crucial behaviour and would do better to observe for longer periods. For scan sampling, the observation is as instantaneous as possible, limited only by how long it takes you to sweep your eyes over the whole group and record what they are doing. But you need to decide how frequently to do this. With focal animal sampling, an observation period of 10–20 minutes is common. However, this is based more on convenience than anything else because 10–20 minutes is a reasonably comfortable time for most people to concentrate. Observing for up to 20 minutes every hour throughout the day still allows you to do other things, such as eat, or get warm, or move between observation sites. If you are going to collect data over a long period of time, there is no point setting yourself such an arduous regime that you fail to complete it. What is comfortable for an observer is therefore not a trivial consideration, but the main factors determining length of sample period should be the duration and the frequency of the behaviour itself (Tyler, 1979; Engel, 1996). Behaviour that lasts a long time (such as a state of lying down for hours), or is very rare (such as only occurring every two days), will require different sample lengths and intervals.

Here we come up against yet another example of Catch 22 in the design of our research protocol. If we *knew* enough about the durations and frequencies of the behaviour to be able to set the length of the observation periods and the intervals between them with any statistical certainty, we would have had to do the observations first. But we don't know how often or for how long they occur, which is why we are planning to do the observations in the first place. The sensible way out of this dilemma is to take the same pragmatic view of the length of time your observation periods should last for as we did for sample size estimates. Do a pilot study and then take a decision based on a reasonable balance between what is likely to enable you to record the behaviour in question and at the same time is a manageable work regime for you. We have yet another role for the preliminary period of watching the animals beforehand.

6.3   Repeated observations on the same animals

One of the cardinal rules in the design of any research protocol is the independence of the data (Principle 1, section 4.1). But we have also seen that

Principle 3 (blocking) states that it can be positively desirable to spend another observation period on the same animal and/or to choose another animal from the same group (section 4. 3). It is therefore crucial to keep in mind the distinction between pseudo-replication and blocking or matching (4. 4). Here is a summary of the various arguments about when you should and should not make repeated observations on the same animals.

There are two good reasons and one bad reason for observing the same animal or animals repeatedly. The first good reason is to improve the *accuracy* of your results (4.1.2). If you observe an animal for only 10 minutes, you might miss some of its behaviour. You might be unlucky and happen to observe it when it was taking a nap when in fact it spent most of the time actively moving around. Since you may not know before you start how accurately 10 minute's worth of time reflects the actual way it spend its life, taking more samples of behaviour might well increase the accuracy with which the samples of time for which you observe it reflect what the animal spends most of its time doing. For example, if you observed the same animal not just once but for 4 different 10 minute periods spread throughout the day, you would have a total observation of 40 minutes rather than 10 from which to calculate the mean duration or frequency of behaviour. You would be much less likely to miss some behaviours because the animal happened to be asleep or only did them at some times of day. Note that, to preserve the independence of your data, you should still end up with one mean per behaviour per animal, not four times as many. You would, in other words, put the same number of independent animals into your analysis, but each sample, being based on more minutes of observation, would be more accurate.

The second good reason for observing the same animals on different occasions is that this may be part of your matched or blocked statistical design (Chapter 4, Principle 3). Given the amount of individual variation in behaviour, repeated observations on the same animal may in fact be one of the best ways of cutting out unwanted variation between individuals and showing up the statistical significance of the effects you are interested in. For example, if you were studying the way a lamb's interactions with its mother changed as it got older, and were using focal animal sampling to measure amount of time spent suckling or amount of time spent within one metre, then it would be part of your hypothesis that there should be consistent changes in the same animal with age (section 4.3.3). There might be quite considerable variation between lambs in how much they interacted with their mothers at a given age but these individual differences are not of interest to you and therefore you need to see that they don't interfere with your main results. The ideal would of course be to have lambs and mothers that all behaved in the same way, but this is impossible, so you have to eliminate the variation between them statistically. The best way to do this would be to regard each lamb-ewe pair as a 'block' (section 4.3.2) and to measure each one at each age. The prediction you would be testing would be that the same lambs behaved differently at different ages. To achieve this, you *must* observe the same animals repeatedly.

Note that here too you have not artificially inflated the number of independent animals in your study. N = the number of independent lamb-ewe pairs and the fact that you may have observed them repeatedly as each pair got older doesn't change that. N is the number of independent life histories of different lambs. By repeatedly observing them, you have increased your knowledge of the life of each one, but you haven't increased the number of lambs.

Armed with an understanding of the two good reasons for making repeated observations, we can now reiterate the bad reason. You cannot make more and more observations on the same animal or the same group in order to pretend that you have increased your sample size. Principle 1 must not be violated, even in the interests of accuracy or to take advantage of blocked designs. A cell biologist might have 30 agar plates lined up in a row on a laboratory bench and regard the colonies as 'independent', but 30 sheep in a field that is much bigger will be so alert to what the others are doing that there that there is no way they can be regarded as 'independent' even if they are all in separate pens. Social behaviour is so much part of the lives of many animals that they can be seen as having *evolved* to be non-independent if they are within sight or sound or smell of each other.

6.4   Increasing independence

True independence in behavioural data is thus often difficult to achieve but at least you can try not to fall into the most obvious traps. Try, if at all possible, to observe animals from different groups that are not in contact with each other. Sometimes, confronted with a single group of rare animals, you may have to take focal samples on different animals within the same group, knowing that this is less than ideal but forced on you by circumstances. Even here there are steps you can take to improve the degree of independence of your data. For example, in observing different animals within the group, make sure that the periods when you observe them are well spaced out so that what has happened in one observation period when you are watching one animal (for example the giving of an alarm call) doesn't spill over and be still affecting the behaviour of the next animal you observe. And you could design your observations so that you randomly chose which animal to observe on a given occasion (section 4.2.3), thereby reducing the chance that you would observe all the boldest animals in the morning and all the timid ones later in the afternoon.

But above all, don't claim too much for observations tinged with non-independence. If all the animals in the same group are infected with the same disease, or terrified by the same dominant animal, or have all learnt from each other how to obtain food in the same way, they are not going to be randomly selected representatives of their species, despite the fact that 50 of them are all showing the same behaviour. Be open about the limitations of your research, particularly where the restrictions on independence have been forced on you by the fact that there were only a certain number of baboons available for you to watch, or the farmer had all his pigs in the same field. You will get more credit from being cautious about the conclusions you can draw than by giving the impression you thought that non-independence was not a problem at all. It may even be necessary to change your research question so that it can be answered with what is available (Chapter 7).

6.5   Recognizing individuals

For some questions—such as whether there are individual differences in behaviour—you clearly need to be able to identify different animals. In other cases, however, it is not necessary to recognize an animal as an individual, particularly if you are randomly choosing a focal animal from a group. With a little practice, you can simply keep your eye on it for the 10 minutes or so of the observation period or the sequence of video. Unless your observational design protocol demands that you identify precisely that animal on another occasion, the animal does not need to be distinguished from any others as long as the next time you observe, you randomly choose again. For many designs it would actually be better to choose another individual, but with unmarked individuals you can't be sure whether you have or have not done so. You may, by chance, choose the same individual twice, but provided that your choice is truly random that should not matter. Such an approach, using repeated random choice of individuals, is particularly suitable for situations where there are large groups of animals all looking alike. Inside commercial chicken houses, for example, there may be thousands of birds together, and marking them individually would be impossible, partly because it would interfere with the behaviour of the animals (chickens are very responsive to visual cues) and partly because the tags would be unacceptable on a commercial product (if they ended up on someone's plate).

Where you do need to identify individuals, there are two options. One is to catch the animals before you start making your observations and mark them in some way, such as with wing tags, leg bands, or collars. The other option is to make use of the fact that many animals are naturally individually distinct in ways that can be used as the basis for recognizing them as individuals. This has the advantage of being non-invasive, non-intrusive, and it is much, much easier because it is already in place. Domestic animals such as ponies are often very distinctive in colour and easy to recognize even at a distance. Gloucester Old Spot pigs come ready made for behaviour projects in which individuals have to be distinguished (Fig. 6.2). Even wild animals are often different enough to be told apart by their distinguishing marks. For example, wild elephants have been reliably distinguished by features such as the pattern of wrinkles on their faces and the blood vessel patterns in their ears (Whitehouse and Hall-Martin, 2000).

There are also good reasons for not marking or tagging animals unless it is absolutely essential. Trapping or darting animals to catch them is always a risk and has obvious welfare implications for the animals. Even when the tags themselves are apparently harmless, they may interfere with behaviour. An extraordinary series of experiments by Burley (1988) showed that the coloured leg bands that she had used to identify individual male zebra finches (*Taeaniopygia guttata*) affected not only their attractiveness to females but also their success as fathers. The females seemed to confuse the red leg bands with the red beaks that males have naturally as a sexual signal.

Fig. 6.2   Gloucester old spot pigs have naturally distinct markings. Photograph by Marian Stamp Dawkins.

It is therefore always worth considering whether artificial marks or tags are absolutely necessary and whether you could get the information you need without them.

6.6 Disappearing animals

Even if you have successfully chosen your animal, identified it, and started to record its behaviour, you may still be faced with the animal flying off or disappearing down a bolt hole before you have had a chance to finish your observational sample. Worse, you may get muddled between two similar looking animals and not be quite sure which one you are supposed to be watching. The only thing to do under such circumstances is to record what happened and when the observation period ended. The record may still be usable. For example, if you were recording the percentage of time an animal spent feeding, you may still be able to salvage that even from a truncated record.

Don't think that this problem would be any less if you were using video or radio tracking. Filmed animals have an annoying habit of walking off camera and radio tracked animals can go entirely off message. You might think that you could counter this, at least for video records, by running the video forward, making sure your chosen animal was on view for the full 10 minutes before you ever started collecting data. You would then be sure of having complete records. But beware. If you did this, you might end up looking at the behaviour of only the most stationary animals, and so a possible bias could creep in. Leaving before they 'should' might actually be a biologically interesting observation about the animals themselves. Suppose that at water-holes, some animals never stayed more than a few minutes, whereas others stayed longer. This might well affect their chances of survival and so would have adaptive significance in its own right. Disappearing after a short time would thus be more than just an annoying event for you. It could be a matter life and death for them.

6.7 Missing animals

Even more disconcerting than animals that disappear while you are watching them are the ones that aren't there at all when your next observation sample is due. Most studies can cope with a few missing observations and there are statistical techniques for doing analyses despite the data sets not being complete, but obviously there are limits beyond which the study would become meaningless. Persistent problems with finding animals to observe should become clear at the preparatory or pilot stage of your observations and should then lead you to change the protocol before you even begin serious observations. If you know you can only guarantee to find your animals once a day when they come to drink, then ask a question that can be answered with once a day observations. Don't even attempt a study that demands you find them throughout the day if this is going to be a regular problem (section 5.4.4).

6.8   Animals responding to the observer

One problem with observational studies is that the animals may be observing you as well as the other way round. They may be afraid of you and fly or run away. Or they may be so interested in you that they spend all their time investigating you. Often sitting quietly for 10–15 minutes before you start recording is enough to remedy both of these situations, but if the problems persist you may need to prevent them seeing you from altogether and use a hide or blind. Sometimes less drastic measures work quite well. Cattle often seem fascinated by human beings (Fig. 6.3) but positioning yourself up a step ladder or a tree, above their line of sight, may result in their ignoring your altogether. Video or CCTV, when you have access to them, may be particularly valuable here.

Fig. 6.3   Cattle are often very curious about human observers, Photograph by Roland Bonney.

6.9   Observer reliability

Some people erroneously refer to behavioural observations as 'subjective', perhaps unfavourably contrasting them with physiological measurements that are said to be 'objective'. As 'subjective' means known only to the person experiencing something, this is not an accurate description of what observers of behaviour do. Two people can see that a bird is pecking the ground or running a wing feather through its beak just as objectively as two people can read a thermometer or measure the concentration of a hormone. What distinguishes behaviour and physiology in the eyes of some people, however, is that they believe that behavioural measurements are less *reliable* than physiological ones, meaning that it is less easy for two people to agree what, say, an 'aggressive peck' is than what a level of a given hormone is. The variability of behaviour, both between individuals of the same species and also within the same individual at different times is often thought to make it difficult to come up with reliable, repeatable measures that can be used in the same way by different observers (section 4.2.8). Other people beg to differ, pointing out that physiological measures, too, exhibit great variability and are often difficult to interpret (Rushen, 1991). Whatever the truth of that argument, the fact remains that the reliability of behavioural (and physiological) measures needs to be checked or validated from time to time. This is particularly true when more than one observer is engaged in a single study, so that *inter-observer reliability* may become an issue, but it also applies when there is just one observer whose criteria for different behaviours may 'slip' as a study proceeds. An easy way to do this is to have two observers independently observe the same animal (or same video clip) and check that they are both recording in the same way. Clear definitions of all behaviour patterns, if possible back up with drawings, photographs or video, help both to explain to other people about your research and to train observers who may be assisting you in the collection of data (section 4.2.3).

6.10   Ethics

Any use of animals potentially raises issues of the ethics involved, even when 'use' here is so remote as to include doing nothing more than watching animals through binoculars. Your very presence in the area may affect the animals, and so there could be ethical issues even about the length of time you spend there or how much you move around. So, as you construct your research protocol, you need to think, at every stage, whether there are ways in which you could reduce your impact on animals, ideally without compromising the research you want to do (ASAB/ABS, 2006). We have already discussed the contribution of sample size to the reduction of animal suffering in research (section 6.1.2), but there are other issues too. Do you have to mark your animals individually or could you do just as valid a study by making use of the naturally occurring variation? (section 6.5). Can you think of less intrusive ways of observing the animals? You may in various ways be able to refine your protocol and so include at least two of the three Rs in what you do. The third R—replacement—is the least likely to apply because if you are studying the behaviour of foxes, say, you can't really replace them with any other species because that is what you are studying.

Application, or at least consideration, of the three Rs should be carried out even if no ethical problems are apparent and no ethical permission needs to be obtained. Obviously, if you do need the permission of a local ethical committee to carry out your work, you need to get this well in advance of the start of your study (Chapter 7). Usually, observers of animal behaviour have the satisfaction of concluding that the reason they are not using any 'alternatives' to what they propose is that any alternatives they can think of inflict much more stress on animals than their observations. Observation *is* an alternative in itself.

6.11 Recording the data

You have yet to take a decision about how to actually record the data. Should you just use a notebook and stopwatch, or would it be better and more accurate to use a small portable computer? What about recording everything on video, camera, or even webcam so that you have a safe and secure record for future analysis? There are sometimes clear advantages in doing this and there are now various software packages available to help you extract information. These include Observer XT (www.com), Jwatcher (www.jwatcher.ucla.edu). EthoLog (www.ip.usp.br/ebottoni/EthoLog/ethohome.html) and Odlog (www.macropodsoftware.com). While there are some projects where video or other automatic recording is essential (for example, day long observations that you physically cannot record directly), there are some surprising advantages of direct observation and the simplest of recording methods. You often see more of the behaviour from direct observation than you do from video, and a notebook and stopwatch are trouble-free inexpensive aids that will take you a long way. As I want to encourage people without access to expensive equipment to observe animal behaviour, I have tried to stress that such equipment is often helpful but that it is not essential. Good design and asking precise, answerable questions are essential in animal behaviour research. Careful observation and analysis of what you observe are what really matter.

Technology is also opening up new possibilities for what we can observe and how we record behaviour (Chapter 10). But there is still a lot that can be done with nothing more than the most minimal equipment, such as notebooks, stop watches, thermometers etc.

There are several different ways of recording behaviour with pen and paper. The simplest is simply to write down the times at which key behaviours stop and start, by glancing at a stopwatch. You will probably find it helpful to have your own abbreviations for each behaviour so that you only have to write down a single letter or at most two for each behaviour. Recording can be made easier and more standardized by preparing data sheets in advance and always recording things in exactly the same way. Fig. 6.4 shows two examples of possible ways in which this can be done, but you will probably want to devise your own data sheets to fit particular situations.

6.12 Recording factors other than behaviour

Whether you record your observations on paper or use video, electronic, or other means of recording, each observation should be labelled by date, time, location, and other details you have decided are important such as weather information, total numbers of animals visible, etc. If you are using paper, a waterproof notebook, or data sheets on a clipboard are useful and it often helps to print out maps and sheets with slots for all the information you intend to record beforehand (Fig. 6.4), so that you don't forget something. If you are using video, you will still need to record on paper the details of when and where the video recordings are being made. Document as much as you can. Keeping good records of exactly what you have done, including departures from your planned protocol, is an essential part of good research.

Obviously if your hypothesis depends on the accurate measurement of some variable such as the amount of ammonia in the air, or light levels, or the state of the tide, then you should choose the appropriate measuring instrument and make sure you can record whenever you make observations. Don't always assume you need expensive instruments because low-tech alternatives are often perfectly adequate and are much less trouble to read and carry around. For example, to measure windspeed you could buy an anemometer, or you could simply use the Beaufort windscale (Appendix 3). To measure light levels you could use a light metre, or you could simply record whether the sun was obscured by cloud or visible. Meteorological measurements can often be obtained from local weather stations or from the internet, even retrospectively.

DATE:

WEATHER: Light breeze sunny

MALE: 4 (white patch)

OBESRVER(S): X, Y

COMMENTS: tractor ploughing in next field

TIME: arrived 10.15

LOCATION: Site X

A.

START TIME:	10.25
Minute	
1	w w w hd
2	hu hd f hu
3	w w
4	w hd f hu
5	w hd f f hu
6	w w
7	hd hu hd f
8	f hu
9	w
10	
END TIME	10.32 (Animals disturbed) moved away

B.

Min	Head up	Head down	Walk	Feed	Drink	Lie
1		✓	✓			
2	✓	✓		✓		
3			✓			
4	✓	✓	✓	✓		
5	✓	✓	✓	✓		
6			✓			
7	✓	✓		✓		
8	✓			✓		
9			✓			
10	Animals disturbed – moved away					

Fig. 6.4 Two possible data sheets for recording behaviour, using a stopwatch. In 'A', you simply write down a letter for each behaviour you see, moving on to the next line after a minute. This gives a zero/one measure of whether or not behaviour has occurred in a given minute and also how often behaviour has occurred within a given time frame. It also enables you to see whether certain behaviours occur together within the same minute. 'B' gives similar data, and is very suitable for zero/one records. I personally find it easier to write down letters without taking my eyes off the animals, but other people find the check sheet method easier.

6.13   The protocol

You are now in a position to write your protocol or detailed research programme, which means a schedule of exactly what observations you will do and when you will do it. Your aim should be to write it in sufficient detail that somebody else could step in, read your instructions, and know exactly what you did.

As there are many different valid ways of planning and carrying out a programme of research, all of which can fulfil the requirements of 'good design', we will take just one example to see how it might be done. You will then be able to see how independence, not confounding variables, and reducing background variation can be achieved in practice, and how your own protocol might be drawn up. The point is not for you to copy this exactly but for you to see, more generally, how you might go about constructing your own.

As an example, we will take a straightforward set of observations undertaken with the aim of asking whether males of a particular species do more of a particular behaviour X than females. X could be anything (grooming, feeding, fighting) but for the sake of argument, let us concentrate on vigilance behaviour. The animals are hypothetical, but to make the design of the observations as easy as possible, we will think of them as deer or a rare breed of cattle kept in large enclosures (so that we can be sure of finding them) but with considerable freedom to move around. They are also obliging enough not to run away when we approach them. We are going to ask, quite simply, whether males are more vigilant than females. This particular project might be part of a longer term investigation into the factors affecting vigilance in males, such as whether it is related to presence of other males, receptiveness of females, whether it varies with season, rank of the male, whether or not he is related to the rest of the group, and so on, but initially we stick to the one question of whether there is an overall difference in the behaviour of males and females.

Taking the list of questions summarized at the end of Chapter 5, we decide that the *level* of observation is the individual animal rather than the whole group and that the *units* of behaviour we will record will be vigilance (= standing with head up alert), feeding (head down), and sitting. A period of watching these animals has shown that most of their time is divided between these three behavioural categories and that it will be relatively easy to record when each of them starts and ends. We decide to use *focal animal sampling* because the groups can be quite large (up to 20) and trying to record numbers with heads up and head down and distinguish the sexes in an instantaneous scan is not going to be possible. We decide to use *continuous* recording throughout the focal sample and using the starting and stopping times for each instance of behaviour will give us information about both the *duration* and *frequency* of vigilance behaviour.

Next, we turn to the issue of *sample size* (section 6.1).We have been lucky enough to locate ten different groups of these animals, all living in geographically separate areas of the country. We can thus treat each group as an independent statistical unit, but this has the disadvantage that no more than one group can be observed in any one day. We have established that each group has both males and females but these are in varying numbers and the total size of the ten groups is also variable. This means we have independent replication, but possibly also considerable variation between the groups caused by the fact that they are in different places, have different numbers of animals in them, and will have to be observed on different days. Will ten groups be a large enough sample size? Without doing more observations first it is impossible to be sure, but our initial observations on just one group suggest that there may be a quite substantial difference between males and females. Males appear to be much more vigilant than females and so a sample size of ten will probably be enough. If it turns out not to be, we can use this first study to guide our choice of sample size in future, using the differences between males and females we observe this time to calculate future sample size more accurately (Fig. 6.2).

We decide on 20 minutes as the *length* of the observational sample and once an hour as the *interval* between samples. This, we know from our observations so far, will give us many different examples of vigilance in both sexes. We decide to observe four males and four females in each group, so that this gives eight observations spaced at hourly intervals across the day, a manageable observation programme, even allowing for travel to and from each site. Males and females turn out to be very easy to distinguish from each other and individuals of both sexes have enough distinguishing marks that we can avoid observing the same individual on two separate occasions. Observing across the day will make sure that our conclusions are not confined to one time of day. Observing four males and four females from each group will improve the accuracy of our results compared to just observing one animal.

We want to end up with a simple comparison: vigilance in males versus vigilance in females. Our hypothesis is that males will be more vigilant with two predictions;

a) males will spend more time (total duration) with 'head up alert' than females;
b) males will raise their heads more often (frequency) than females.

The independence of the ten groups allows us to use 'group' as the unit of replication. The observations on the four males and four females at each site will be combined into a male mean and and a female mean. We aim for data in the following form:

Group 1	M	F	Location 1	Day 1
Group 2	M	F	Location 2	Day 2
Group 3	M	F	Location 3	Day 3
Group 4	M	F	Location 4	Day 4
Group 5	M	F	Location 5	Day 5
Group 6	M	F	Location 6	Day 6
Group 7	M	F	Location 7	Day 7
Group 8	M	F	Location 8	Day 8
Group 9	M	F	Location 9	Day 9
Group 10	M	F	Location 10	Day 10

Now, these ten groups are all very different. Not only are they living in different places, but the total number of animals in each varies. Some groups have more males than females, some have equal numbers. Some have only adults over a year old, some have young born this year. Also, the fact that we have to observe the groups on different days is going to mean that the weather may be quite different when we observe them.

Once you may have thought that all these differences would make it quite impossible to obtain any valid data at all. But I hope that by now you can see that this is not true and that we can invoke Principle 3 of good design and use blocking or matching as a way of not letting the differences get in the way of what we really want to know—namely whether males differ from females. The design we are going to adopt is a blocked design, where males or females at the same location are matched or blocked (Chapter 4, section). The 'blocks' are animals in the same group, in the same place, and observed on the same day as each other.

We will be comparing male and female behaviour separately at each location (where of course all these other factors such as group size, and weather, and day of observing are the same). We ask, for each location, is male behaviour different from female behaviour? Does the sex difference hold up *despite* all the other variation? If males are consistently more vigilant than females, whether they are found in a large group and it is a bright sunny day or they are found in a small group several miles away on a rainy day, then that suggests that the sex difference is real. It is strong enough and persistent enough to show up despite all the other things that are also differing between our ten groups. Statistically, we have separated 'block' variance (between groups) from the interesting variance (between the sexes).

Strictly speaking, of course, we do not know whether any variation that shows up between the different locations is because the ten groups of animals are themselves intrinsically different, or because we observed them in different places, or because we observed them on different days. But the source of the difference does not matter if the main question is about differences between males and females. We have respected Principle 2 (not confounding variables) in the sense that we have not confounded differences between the sexes with any of the other differences between the locations.

There is, however, another potential violation of Principle 2 lurking in the background. We want to compare or match males and females at a given location in such a way that there are no other possible differences between them (apart from their sex), but as we have only one pair of eyes and one pair of hands, we cannot observe focal animals of both sexes simultaneously. If we always chose to observe males first, we run the risk of confounding the order of observation with the difference between males and females. So we need to balance or randomize the order in which we observe males and females. For the reasons given in Chapter 4, we will set up our protocol as a balanced design, so that at each location, there will be four 20 minute observations in the morning (two on males; two on females), and four similar observations in the afternoon:

8 am	Observe Female for 20 mins
9 am	Observe Male for 20 mins
10 am	Observe Male for 20 mins
11 am	Observe Female for 20 mins
12 pm	Observe Female for 20 mins
1 pm	Observe Male for 2 0 mins
2 pm	Observe Male for 20 mins
3 pm	Observe Female for 20 mins

We now have to decide exactly which male and which female to observe at any one time. We decide to choose an animal at random (using the acetate sheet method—section 4.2.3). Just before each observation session, an animal of the required sex will be chosen. If it has been observed before that day, another random choice will be made. Pilot studies showed that the animals appear to take little notice of us as an observer (section 6.8) but, to be on the safe side, we decide to take up position ten minutes before each observation session to make sure we disturb them as little as possible. For each location, we record the size of the group and the total numbers of males and females, as well other information about the site that may be relevant such as presence or absence of cover, feeding times, locations of roads etc. For each individual observation we plan to record: the number of animals visible, the weather, time, temperature, wind speed and direction, and other information about the location, and we design our data sheets appropriately (section 6.12).

So, reviewing our plans for the programme of observations, we can see that the *independence* of the data is ensured by the fact that there are ten groups, all isolated from one another. The *non-confounding of variables* is reduced as much as possible by the order in which the males and females are to be observed, the fact that the same observer will take all the observations in a standard way, and the fact that the animals to be observed will be chosen at random from those available. And *blocking* is being used to eliminate statistically a large amount of unwanted or nuisance variation such as the fact that not all the groups are the same size, or in the same place, variation that we cannot eliminate in any other way.

I must stress here, however, that this is only one of many different possible ways of designing such a study, even just for the one question about the difference in vigilance behaviour between males and females. There are, in fact, a number of more complex designs than this one that you could use. The point is not that you must adopt this design or even anything like it. The point is that this is the *kind* of exercise you need to go through before you carry out any observational (or indeed, experimental) study. Much of it is common sense. Common sense will also enable you to adopt the design best fitted to your particular project. All I have attempted to do is to approach observational design in the most basic and simple way so that you get a feel for what needs to be taken into consideration and where you are most likely to go wrong. You can always learn about more advanced designs and statistical analysis later on (Grafen and Hails, 2002, McCleery et al., 2007).

6.14   Pilot studies

You should now be able to draw up a detailed research protocol and have made decisions about:

1) the number of independent statistical units in your study (sample size);
2) the number and type of observational samples you will take from each independent unit;
3) the length and interval between these samples;
4) whether you will be doing repeat observations on the same animal;
5) whether you need to be able to recognize individuals and if so, how you will do it;
6) the order in which you will observe different animals.

Once you think you have a workable protocol, *try it out* and see whether it works in practice. There is no substitute for having a trial run to find out if what you plan to do is manageable, possible, and is going to be worth the investment of your time and energy. Spend a little time seeing that everything is running smoothly. Are your data sheets convenient or could they be improved? Can you reliably see the behaviour you want to record? Have you left yourself enough time to move between one study site and the next?

If everything seems to be working, you may now think that all you have to do is to put everything in your rucksack and set off to make your observations. Surely now, after all this preparation, you are ready to collect the data that will, finally, put your hypothesis to the test. Well, you might be ready. You might have a very clear idea of what you would, ideally, like to do. But what do other people think? How does what you want to do fit in with the routine of a farmer, the resources of a zoo, or what else is happening in the wood where you want to work? Before you can translate your proposal, however good and however well it fits the requirements of good design, into the reality of data collection, you have one further but essential stage in your planning. You have to make contact with the other people who will be affected by your work and do a 'reality check'. Is what you want to do feasible, within budget and logistically possible? Have you obtained permission where it is needed? Will the animals be available when you want them? Will you, in other words, be able to implement your project in practice? The next chapter is about making your project happen in the less than ideal worlds of agriculture, zoos, the countryside, and the great awkward, inconvenient world we all live in.

7 Observing in farms, in zoos, and in the wild

Sometimes it will seem as though circumstances have conspired to make it impossible for you to carry out your study in the way that you would ideally like to. Some of these circumstances will emerge at the design or pilot study stages, such as not being able to find enough animals to make your data truly independent. Others will be problems that you did not foresee at all but which are enough to threaten the success of even the best designed study. These include animals that get ill or are unexpectedly sent off to slaughter before you have finished your study; animals that tamper with, eat, step on, or run off with bits of your equipment; forest fires; dogs; disease epidemics; and members of the public asking you what you are doing. These categories are not distinct. The 'unexpected' removal of animals by a farmer before you had completed your observations could have been anticipated had you discussed your plans with him beforehand, and either come to some agreement about when the animals were to be moved or planned shorter observations that fitted in with his programme. In this chapter, we will look at some of the things you can do to minimize the risks of your study going wrong by anticipating problems before they happen and, if necessary, taking pre-emptive action so that they do not ruin your study.

7.1 Observational design meets the real world

Whenever your study involves any other person, even if it is only obtaining their permission to observe from a particular place, it is essential that you consult them at a very early stage to find out what you can and cannot do. It is no good planning a study that involves night-time watches in a wood if you are not going to be allowed into the wood at night. It is no good planning a study that involves twenty independent replicates of chimpanzee behaviour if the head keeper could easily tell you that there is only one group of five chimpanzees in the entire zoo. Remember that farmers and zoo owners are trying to run commercial businesses and although they may be very helpful and very interested in what you are doing, they have limited time and resources. Don't expect them to do lots of things for you, such as marking animals that weren't going to be marked anyway or moving animals from one place to another, unless you actually have the financial resources yourself to compensate them. If they offer, fine. But regard this as a bonus, not something you should expect. The first rule of planning an observational study is therefore: *find out what is available* and the second rule is: make *the best use of what is available*.

The third rule is: *if your hypothesis demands something that isn't available in order to test it, then either take steps to make it available or choose another hypothesis to test.* There may be some questions that you might like to ask but can't with the resources and animals you have, and you are much better advised to work within the limitations of what is available and do it well, than be too ambitious and do a fatally flawed study.

7.2   Find out what is available

The obvious things to find out when you are planning a study are how many animals are available, in what groups and of what ages, sexes, breeds etc. You also need to know whether they have individual marks or can be marked and how long they are going to be available. You need to find out how close to them you can get, whether your presence is likely to be disruptive (to the animals or to other people), and whether anyone else is likely to be working in the same area. Knowing the daily routines of farms and zoos, such as when the animals are fed, will help you to plan when to do your observations, as will knowing if there are particular times when wild animals come to watering or feeding places. Obviously if you need to obtain local permits to enter particular places, or permission from landowners, that needs to be initiated at an early stage so that everything is in place when you want to start work.

As a result of talking to the people concerned, you may realize that there is a serious mismatch between what you had planned to do and what you are actually going to be able to do in practice. Some of the commonest problems are:

• *Not enough independent replication (Chapter 4)*

You had thought the animals were in separate pens but they have recently been put into one large group, or they are in pens but they can all see and hear each other. Or, your study depended on there being a large number of sows all giving birth at the same time, but there will only be a few litters born over the period you have available to do the study.

- *You can't recognize individuals (Chapter 4)*

Even after several practice sessions, you still cannot reliably tell the animals apart. The animals have some natural variation in their markings or they have farm tags, but these are not always visible.

- *You can't see what the animals are doing*

Your study depends on being able to record feeding behaviour, but all you can see is whether the animal pecks or pokes into the grass. You can't tell whether it successfully finds something to eat or not.

I am sure you will encounter other problems of your own! Some (such as when piglets are scheduled to be born) are probably non-negotiable. For others (such as whether animals could be marked), it may be possible to discuss various possible options. Do, however, be open-minded in your discussions with the owner or keeper of the animals and realize that what you are suggesting might cause difficulties. Asking to have extra marks put on the animals, for instance, might cause the behaviour of the animals to change, and catching the animals to mark them could be disruptive and cause stress. A constructive alternative may be to ask yourself whether it is absolutely essential to your study that you know the identity of the animals (section 6.5).

7.3　Make the best use of what is available

Be on the lookout for opportunities. You may not be able to carry out the project you had planned to do, but you might be able to do an even better one, or do the original one in an improved way. People in charge of animals, or those who have studied them before, may be able, with very little effort on their part, to provide you with a mine of information that will open up a whole new range of possibilities about the questions you can ask. If there are records already available about the life histories of the animals you plan to study, then these may provide you with ideas for what you might observe or even data that could be incorporated into your study. For example, you might use a farmer's records about how many litters a sow has previously had in your study of sow–piglet interactions to ask whether more experienced sows which had had many litters behaved differently from those that were giving birth for the first time.

A farmer might also be able to tell you that although he has only limited numbers of a certain species, he has neighbours who have more, so you might end up with a much larger sample size than you originally thought was possible. Forest wardens, farm managers, and zoo keepers often have a deep knowledge of their animals' behaviour gathered from many years of watching them and living with them and this too can be a resource. They may be able to help with the observations, at times that are inconvenient for you, for example. Time spent talking to the other people affected by your study can pay great dividends both in terms of what you can do and also in how easily you will be able to do it. Be imaginative and creative about what you can do.

Zoos across the world are now developing ways of combining data from several different institutions (www.biaza.org.uk; www.waza.org; www.easa.net). Even if one zoo has only a limited number of animals, perhaps all kept together in one enclosure, effective sample size can be increased by combining data on the same species from different places (Shepherdson et al., 1998). Each zoo is seen as an independent replicate, and the differences between the zoos can be used to identify factors in the animals' upbringing and environment that may be responsible for differences in the animals' behaviour (Crockett, 1991; Hosey, 1997; Clubb and Mason, 2004). Martin's (2005) study on the effect that being reared without a mother has on the social behaviour of adult chimpanzees, is another good example of making full use of available information (section 2.4). The differences in rearing conditions between the different chimpanzees in different zoos might have been dismissed as making any comparisons impossible. However, Martin used them as an integral part of the study to provide information about the effect of rearing conditions on adult social behaviour, information that it would have been difficult to obtain in any other way.

7.4 If your hypothesis demands something that isn't available to test it, then choose another hypothesis (or test another of its predictions)

If this book has done its job properly, then you will now know about the different kinds of questions that can be asked about animal behaviour and will be in a position to match them up with what is available to achieve high standards of observational research. I hope you will have developed a habit of thinking that seeks out the problems with every research proposal, sees what is needed, and then quite ruthlessly asks whether valid results will really be explained if the research were carried out in the way that is proposed. If they cannot, and there would be serious methodological flaws in the data collected, you should by now be able to take the next step and switch the direction of your research. As there are many different kinds of question that can be asked and many different kinds of evidence that can be collected, a problem with one project does not have to be the end of your research on that topic. On the contrary, there are so many different questions you could ask that all it may take is a bit of imagination to see what possibilities there are. Perhaps you cannot, with what is available, test an adaptive hypothesis, but perhaps you could ask a question about causation or development. Perhaps you cannot use continuous focal animal sampling but you could use *ad lib* sampling. Perhaps you cannot mark each individual animal but you could ask questions about the behaviour of 'anonymous' animals within a group. If you have appreciated the importance of good design to all research, then you will give it the highest priority, even if it means abandoning the project you set out to do in the first place. You would then not be defeated by circumstances but open to opportunities. You should change course not with the intention of doing something inferior but with a view to making sure that what you do is designed to the highest standards. By matching your question to what is available and what other people say is possible, you may end up doing research that has much greater application to the real world than your initial ideas had been.

7.5   The really unexpected

Of course, there will be some occasions when, despite your best laid plans and your most ardent efforts to anticipate the worst that could happen, something even worse does happen. Your animals simply disappear from the area they have been known to inhabit for years, for example. Or your car breaks down on the way to observe your animals so that a whole day's observations are lost. There are statistical ways of dealing with small numbers of 'missing data' (essentially filling them in by guesswork from the data you do have) but there are severe limits on how many holes there can be in your data before it becomes invalid. By definition, you can't do anything about the really unexpected except to try to salvage what you can. Accidents and disasters do happen. But there are two main ways that you can reduce the totally unexpected to a manageable minimum.

Firstly, by thinking ahead and anticipating the things most likely to go wrong, you ward off all but the real disasters. Above all, talk to anyone who might be affected by your project so that they know what you want to achieve and what you need from them. A farmer may still choose to cut his hedges on one of the days you were trying to observe the behaviour of sheep but he is much more likely to postpone his hedge-cutting if you had discussed your project with him and involved him in the outcome. Having a detailed research protocol (section 6.13) is always a help, too. If you know precisely how many days you need for your observations and exactly when and where you will be doing them, you will be able to tell other people, who can then make their own plans accordingly.

Secondly, by doing a 'pilot' study and trying out your protocol in advance, you know what is and is not feasible before you start doing serious observations (section 6.14). You will then minimize your chances of being caught out by the logistics of your study because you already know what does and does not work. The following steps will ensure that you have done what you can to give your observations the greatest possible chance of success:

1) contact other people affected by your study at the earliest possible stage;
2) keep them informed and involved;
3) find out what is available;
4) make the best use of what is available;
5) be prepared to modify your research in the interests of good design;
6) make sure permits and permissions are obtained before you start.

8 Analysing observations

'Success' does not necessarily mean that your observations support your hypothesis or that the animals behave exactly as your predictions said they should. It means that you have rigorously tested the hypothesis and correctly analysed the results so that you know, one way or the other, whether the hypothesis fits the facts. Of course, you can't help feeling pleased if the results do turnout as you predicted, particularly if you had predicted something unusual that everyone else had thought was highly unlikely to be true. And you can't help feeling disappointed if predictions do not seem to be borne out in practice. But results that do not support your hypothesis are valuable too. I once spent a whole summer trying to convince a student that her 'negative' results were really very exciting. She was very disappointed that she had not only failed to find an effect she was looking for, but that the results actually suggested the opposite of what she had predicted, although they were 'not significant' in the wrong direction. Happily, the examiners awarded her a very high mark for her project report, despite the 'negative' results. She had made a genuine step forward by so conclusively showing that the original hypothesis was probably wrong.

So when you come to analyse your results, you need not worry if the predictions you made turn out to be correct or not. If they are, great. If they are not, that is still progress. This chapter takes a preliminary look at how you can go about analysing your observations. It is preliminary rather than comprehensive because the possible ways of analysing observational data is now very great and a full discussion would be way beyond the scope of this book. All this chapter can do, therefore, is to discuss some basic issues that confront anyone whatever type of observational (or experimental) data they have and whatever type of statistical analysis they finally decide to do. These include basic ideas about what it means for results to be 'significant', the difference between parametric and non-parametric tests, and how to choose the right statistical test for your kind of data. But before you do any statistical analysis at all, you need to take one more very important step. You have to prepare and organize your data.

8.1 Organizing data

Your data may have been collected on check-sheets or maps, written in notebooks, or transcribed from video. It may have been spoken into a sound recorder, or typed into a field computer. It may consist of light meter readings, weather reports, or details of animal histories given to you by a farmer or zoo keeper (Chapter 7). You may still have a pile of videotapes yet to be looked at.

Whatever the state of your data and whatever medium it is in, you now need to get it into a form where you can test your predictions. This does not mean a big list of everything you have seen. It means constructing condensed lists of data that can be fed directly into a statistical package. With the simple project design we developed in Chapter 6, for example, we wanted to see whether there were any differences in vigilance behaviour between males and females, but the data were actually collected in a balanced order, with males and females 'mixed up'. The data were also in the form of the exact times when animals lowered and raised their heads during a 20 minute period, whereas what we need is total vigilance times as well as numbers of times animals raised their head. The observations have to be considerably 'tidied up' before they are usable.

We chose to measure 'vigilance' as the total duration of time with head up and alert during a focal 20 minute sample and also as the number of times the head was raised. For each focal animal record, therefore, we need to calculate these two values. If you had used a field recorder for your observations or had analysed video with special software, then you will be able to extract this information automatically. If your data is in the form of written records, you will need to derive this information either manually (using the times between each head up and the next head down) or using a computer programme. Either way, it is a good idea to put your data into a spreadsheet such as Excel. You can then see the data from each animal and each set of observations in a systematic way. You can see whether you have any missing values and you can prepare the data, for example, by calculating the mean for each set of observations if that is what you have decided is going to be your independent statistical unit. You can also insert other information about each block such as group size, group composition, weather, time of observations, and anything else you wish. You can either directly import or cut and paste the prepared data into a statistical package.

8.2 Descriptive statistics

Having your data in the form of a spreadsheet also allows you to get a preliminary idea of what your data are showing you even before you have carried out any sort of statistical tests on it. Just looking at the means and standard deviations of the male and female vigilance behaviour, for example, might show that the results are certainly consistent with the hypothesis that females feed for more time than males. I am constantly amazed by students who rush into my room in a state of great excitement because they have found a 'significant' result, and when I ask whether the results were in the predicted direction they have no idea. So do some simple descriptive statistics, such as calculating the mean and standard deviation of your results and plot them out as a graph. Standard statistical packages will draw such graphs for and you can then see whether your observations on one group are going to give you larger or smaller values than your observations on another group. After all, this is the form in which you will probably present your results to other people and, even at this early stage, you will have an idea of what the results are likely to be.

8.3 Hypothesis testing and 'significance'

All statistical tests involve testing a specific hypothesis (sometimes referred to as H_1) against an alternative. H_1 might be the hypothesis that males are more vigilant than females. But what is the rival or alternative hypothesis that it is to be tested against? It may seem that there is no obvious rival hypothesis, but in fact, there is always a rival, even if it is just the 'null' hypothesis (H_0). H_0 is the hypothesis that there is no difference between males and females. The no difference or null hypothesis is important because in order to show that there is a 'significant' difference between males and females (our predicted hypothesis), we have to be sure that the null hypothesis (no difference) could not have predicted the same result as we actually obtained by chance (section 4.3). Even if you had followed all the rules for randomly selecting males and females to observe, it could still turn out that, purely by chance, you happened to pick females that looked up for atypically longer than average and males that looked up for atypically short periods. If you had randomly selected other individuals to observe, you might have obtained a completely different result. The null hypothesis can sometimes—purely by the luck of the draw affecting which animals are chosen—produce the same result as a genuine difference between males and females, in just the same way that an unbiased coin can sometimes produce whole sequences of heads purely by chance. The role of a statistical test is to distinguish these chance effects from genuine differences between male and female vigilance behaviour or genuinely biased coins. The question we have to ask is: how likely is the null hypothesis to have produced the observed result?

If the answer is 'very unlikely', then we refer to the result as 'statistically significant'. 'Very unlikely' is usually taken to mean that there is only 1 chance in 100 ($p = 0.01$). 'Very, very unlikely' (highly statistically significant') means that there is only 1 chance in 1,000 ($p = 0.001$) that the result could be explained as chance sampling effects under the null hypothesis. The lower the 'p' value, the more highly significant the results are taken to be and the more confident you can be that your results could not be explained by the null hypothesis. You can then start believing that your own hypothesis (H_1) might be true. On the other hand, it is worth noting that a commonly used significance value ($p = 0.05$) means that there is less than 1 chance in 20 that the result could have occurred by chance. That sounds fine until you turn it round and realize that what that really means is that, for every 20 apparently significant results you get, on average 1 of them will be due to chance. For this reason, the level of significance is also referred to as a Type I error: the probability that you will wrongly conclude there is a difference when, in reality, there is no difference at all.

Everything thus hangs on being able to calculate these 'p' values accurately. Fortunately, there are plenty of statistical packages (e.g. Minitab, SSPS and even Excel) that do the actual calculations for you, but you have to be sure that you have fed the correct data into them, in the correct form, and asked the computer to do the right test.

8.3.1 Which statistical test?

The right statistical test for your data is determined first and foremost by the type of measurements you have made (section 5.5) and by the kinds of sampling decisions you made at the design stage (Chapter 6). In the example of the vigilance behaviour, we took measurements of duration, which are *interval measurements* (section 5.5), in form of *continuous samples*. This means that we obtained actual measures or parameters, measured in minutes or seconds. A duration of four minutes is precisely twice as long as a duration of two minutes. With such measurements or parameters, we can use either parametric or non-parametric tests (see next section).

If we had not measured durations so precisely, we might have collected data in the form of ordered or ranked measurements (section 5.5). For example, we might have recorded whether animals were either very vigilant (1 = looking up for 15 minutes or more of an observation sample), moderately vigilant (2 = looking up for between 5 and 15 minutes), or not vigilant (3 = less than 5 minutes). We can still say that one animal was more vigilant than another, but not how much more because having a score of 2 rather than 1 does not mean that one animal was exactly twice as vigilant as another. We can still use these ordered or ranked scores to compare males and females, but we have to use one of the ordered or ranked statistical tests, such as the Wilcoxon matched pairs test, to do so (Fig. 8.1). Yet another way of collecting data would have been to use a categorical zero/one score, such as 'vigilant' (= looked up more than 10 times in 20 minutes) versus 'not vigilant' (= looked up less than 10 times in 20 minutes). A corresponding categorical test, such as the Binomial test, is then needed to analyse the data (Siegel and Castellan, 1998).

Group 1		Group 2
31		18
30		17
25		16
17		11
9		10
8		7
8		10
10		6
Mean = 17.25		Mean = 11.875
Standard deviation = 10.02		Standard deviation = 4.50
	Paired t test shows t = 2.57, which is **significant** at p < 0.05, 2 tailed	
Median = 13.5	Wilcoxon Matched Pairs test shows T+ = 30 which is **not significant** (p > 0.05, 2-tailed)	Median = 10.5

Fig. 8.1   Illustration of how the same set of data can show a 'significant' difference by one test (parametric paired t test) but 'not significant' under a different but less powerful test (non-parametric Wilcoxon matched pairs test). The power of a statistical test (section 6.1) is its ability to demonstrate a significant difference between two sets of measurements when there really is a difference between the groups from which the measurements were taken. Less powerful tests are more liable to what are called Type II errors (failing to show a difference when there really is one there). Generally, the power of any statistical test, parametric nor non-parametric, can be increased by increasing the sample size.

8.3.2   Parametric and non-parametric tests

Because the data we chose to collect were interval data measurements, we had precise measures of durations of looking up and we can use a whole range of powerful statistical tests known as parametric statistics. Parametric statistics are the most widely used of statistical tests and are the ones you are most likely to come across. They have a number of advantages and a number of drawbacks for behavioural data.

The main advantage of parametric statistics is that they are more *powerful* in the sense of being more likely to show up a statistically significant difference if it is really there (Appendix 2). We can illustrate this by applying the parametric t-test and the non-parametric Wilcoxon matched pairs test to the same data set (Fig. 8.1). The parametric t-test yields a statistically significant (p < 0.05) difference at in the vigilance of males and females in duration of looking up. However, the non-parametric test Wilcoxon fails to achieve that level of significance on exactly the same set of data. The Wilcoxon test is less powerful, which makes it more liable to fail to find small but genuine differences between groups (what is known as a Type II error). On the other hand, if a non-parametric test tells you that there is a statistically significant effect, you can be confident that it really is there.

The second advantage, particularly of more complex parametric statistical tests such as the 'analysis of variance', is that they provide information about the relative importance of different factors and of interactions between them. In our discussion of blocks or mini-experiments in a field with varying types of soil (section 4.3), we saw how blocking did not just reveal the effects of different fertilizers despite the field not being uniform, it also had the possibility of showing that fertilizer 'A' might be better than 'B' in the damp end of the field, but less good or even worse than 'B' at the drier well-drained end. Documenting the effects of the different conditions in the field was actually part of the experiment. Such interactions are only possible with parametric tests and interval measurements. There are no non-parametric tests that give such detailed information about so many different factors all at once. Some of the non-parametric tests have somewhat misleading names such as 'Friedman analysis of variance' (Siegel & Costellan, 1998), but these do not do what a real analysis of variance does. They allow you to deal with more than two groups, such as animals at more than two ages, but they do not employ the full power that comes from being able to analyse or partition variance quantitatively (section 4.3). For that, you need parametric statistics. If you can use parametric statistics, it is always a good idea to try to do so, but there is one very important proviso.

You cannot use parametric statistics—even for interval measurements—unless your data satisfy certain criteria. In particular, the variance of the two groups has to be the same and you need to show that all the data have been drawn from a population whose distribution is normal or bell-shaped. Before using a parametric test, you should therefore make sure your data meets these criteria (Grafen and Hails, 2002). Even if your data do not initially meet the criteria, however, you may still be able to use parametric tests if you *transform* the data first, by using the logarithm, arcsine, or square root of the raw data (Sokal and Rohlf, 1969; Grafen and Hails, 2002).

With behaviour, we often find that data do not satisfy the criteria for parametric tests, which is why non-parametric tests, for all their lack of power, are so useful in behavioural work. Non-parametric statistical tests make no assumptions whatever about the distribution of the data or its variance so there no need to transform it, whatever it is. Non-parametric tests can be used to analyse the kind of data that parametric statistics find it difficult or impossible to deal with, such as ordered or rank data, behaviour scored by its intensity, percentages, proportions, or data where there is a ceiling on the maximum value a variable can take (for example because observations were terminated after a set length of time). *Non-parametric Statistics for the Behavioural Sciences* (Siegel and Castellan, 1988) gives a comprehensive account of how to use non-parametric tests and when to use them.

8.4 Some frequently used tests

The six statistical tests you are most likely to use are:
For *categorical* (yes/no) measurements:

(i) *The Binomial test*: for comparing categories such as the numbers of animals choosing option 'A' versus the numbers choosing option 'B'.
(ii) *Chi-square test*: for comparing two or more categories.

For *ordered or rank* measurements:

(iii) *Wilcoxon matched pairs test*: for comparing two matched groups, including comparing animals with themselves under two conditions.
(iv) *Mann-Whitney test*: for comparing two groups that are not matched or blocked.
(v) *Friedman two-way analysis of variance*: for comparing three or more matched or blocked groups.

For *interval* measurements: (iii)–(v) plus:

(vi) *t-test*: paired t-test for comparing two matched groups; unpaired t-test for unmatched groups).
(vii) *Analysis of Variance*: a powerful and flexible way of analysing data.

You should consult a statistician or statistical textbook to guide you in your choice of test.

8.5 Presenting your results

Communicating the results of your research to other people, whether it is in the form of a talk, a publication, a project report, or a poster, is an essential part of the research process. Observational studies often have an immense advantage in this respect, as reports can be illustrated with photographs of the animals or the picturesque places in which they have been studied. But above all, pictures or no pictures, your report must tell a story, the story of what you did.

The story begins with an *Introduction*, explaining why you undertook the study in the first place and what was important about the question or questions you set out to answer. You need to explain enough about the background of the project that people can see why it is interesting but also what is currently missing or unknown or unclear. At this point, you can stress the importance of your own study as an attempt to fill the gaps in existing knowledge. You should be quite explicit about this. Somewhere early on in the introduction should be a sentence with some version of the words 'the aim of this project was to . . . ' or even 'we here show that . . . '. This is a *signpost* to the rest of the paper, a reassurance to the reader that they understand what the research was all about and why it was important. You should state the hypothesis clearly and list the predictions you are going to test. Number the predictions and describe in broad terms how you set about testing them. This gives the impression that you really know what you are talking about and that it is going to be worth reading the rest of the paper.

The *Methods* section should include a description of how you carried out the research and, like the protocol you drew up for your own observations, contain enough detail for the reader to be able to visualize exactly what you did and to be able replicate it for themselves. It should even include a description of the things that went wrong, of the pilot studies that didn't turn out the way you though they would and made you change the way you eventually carried out the study. *Statistical methods* should be described as a sub-section of the *Methods*, as should *ethical issues* you addressed or permissions you obtained.

The story should continue with a clear description of the *Results* of your study. When you have a lot of different results, it is a good idea to list them in the same order as you listed the predictions you were making so that the reader can see which ones were upheld and which were not. If you had three predictions in the *Introduction*, you could then have three sub-sections in your results, each labelled with its corresponding prediction. There is no need to give all the raw data (although you may want to include this in an appendix or web-based section), but you should try and summarize the main findings succinctly so that the reader knows what the 'take-home message' is. Use graphs and figures to make it as easy as possible for your reader to understand what you found. Experiment with different ways of presenting your data. For example, a combined graph with histograms of different colours might be more effective than many small graphs.

Finally, the *Discussion* should describe where the research has got to, what is known now that was not known before you started, and which of the results are the most important. You need to include a critical evaluation of what you have done and which results need to be treated with caution or need more data. At the end of the story, you might point to the next steps that need to be taken. The *Discussion* should pick up the same points that you signposted in the *Introduction*—the predictions that were tested and did or did not fit what you observed, and what this now says about our current state of knowledge of the whole subject. How has your study moved our knowledge forward? Are your results different from those of other people and, if so, how might you explain this? Did your observations yield some completely unexpected results? Might this suggest a completely new hypothesis?

Above all, make it easy for your reader to understand and remember what you have found. You cannot go too far wrong if you model your report on papers already published in journals such as *Animal Behaviour* and use the *Guidelines for authors* in that or other behaviour journals. Obviously, in preparing the manuscript for publication, you need to stick closely to the instructions for the particular journal you will send your manuscript to. Take this part of the research seriously. The reporting of your observations and the communication of what you have discovered to other people is the only way in which they will ultimately contribute to our understanding of animal behaviour.

9 Further observations

We have now covered the basic elements of how to observe animal behaviour. To make it as clear as possible what each stage in this process involves, I have deliberately concentrated on just one kind of measurement: that of *how much* behaviour an animal does. I wanted to emphasize the continuity of the whole process of conceiving, designing, and carrying out observations, and to show that the appropriate statistical analysis is determined by decisions that have already been made at the design stage. If you have decided to go for a blocked design, you will already have destined your observations for a certain kind of analysis, for example, and if you have recorded data on a ranked scale, you will have to analyse them with non-parametric tests. I felt that this message, of the interplay between different parts of the observational process, was best conveyed by using a single example and following it through from one stage to the next. But in focusing on a comparison of how much vigilance is shown by males and females, I do not want to give the impression that all observational studies have to follow exactly the same format or even that there is only one kind of analysis you can do on data collected in this way. There are many other ways of analysing behaviour and many other questions you can ask. In this chapter, we will explore some of these other possible approaches and look at some of the additional analyses you can do and measurements you can make that will greatly increase the scope of your observations. The chapter does not even pretend to be comprehensive. For more detailed treatments see Lehner (1996) and Martin and Bateson (1993). Here, we will look at just a few examples chosen to show what can be done with the simplest of equipment. The aim is to inspire you as to what you might be able to do yourself.

9.1   When behaviour occurs: intervals

Observational samples of the sort we have already discussed (Chapter 5) are building blocks that can then be assembled in a variety of different ways to answer a variety of additional questions about behaviour. One of the most important of these is to provide information about the timing of behaviour—that is, *when* behaviour occurs. If you consistently sample in exactly the same way at different times of day, year, or whatever time scale you are interested in, you can build the observations into a complete picture of how behaviour varies with time. For example, hourly scan samples on the numbers of free-range broiler (meat) chickens seen outside their houses over the course of a day showed a clear diurnal rhythm (Fig. 9.1). Many more birds came outside in the early morning and in the evening than at midday (Dawkins et al., 2003).

Focal samples can similarly be assembled into analyses of how behaviour varies with time. In our previous analysis, we took the mean duration per sample (section 5.7.2), which would allow us to have a summary measure of behaviour for each time of day. However, by adding up all the individual durations of behaviour within a sample, we inevitably lost a lot of valuable information about exactly when each instance of behaviour occurred. An alternative way of analysing the same data would be to deliberately disregard total duration and look instead at the *intervals* between successive occurrences of the same behaviour within a sample. To illustrate this, we will take a controversy about the adaptive significance of patterns of vigilance in prey animals, and show how different hypotheses can stand or fall on observations on the timing of behaviour, as measured by intervals between them.

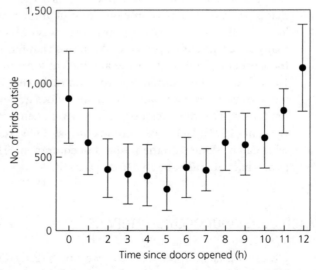

Fig. 9.1 Numbers of free-range broiler chickens seen outside at different times of the day. Each point represents the combined means for spring and summer observations for 14 separate houses. Vertical bars are standard deviations. (From Dawkins et al., 2003)

Pulliam (1973) proposed a specific time interval hypothesis for the behaviour of animals that both feed and keep watch for predators at the same time. His hypothesis applied particularly to animals that cannot see their surroundings while they feed, such as birds that peck into long grass and so have to stop feeding periodically to look around for danger. Pulliam argued that the optimum way for such animals to protect themselves would be to look up at random intervals and for random lengths of time, because this would make it most difficult for predators to take them unawares. If the birds raised their heads at random, Pulliam argued, predators would not be able to predict when the birds would next look up there and would be no predictable safe period in which they could approach. If, on the other hand, a bird always left a predictable interval between looking down and looking up again, the predators could learn that they had this amount of time to creep up unobserved, like criminals using the predictable behaviour of security guards away on a routine patrol to give them a window of opportunity.

Subsequently, however, the generality of Pulliam's hypothesis has been questioned (Bednekoff and Lima, 1998; Cresswell et al., 2003). It only works if predators time their attacks with respect to what the prey are doing, like the criminals watching the security guards for the right moment. If the predators make no distinction between prey with their heads up and those with their heads down feeding, there is no point in the prey scanning at random. The prey should look up at constant intervals and for a constant time, both of these constants being the ones that give them the best chance of detecting danger. The constants might vary depending on conditions, such as light levels, but on a given occasion they should approach an optimum—there should be one 'best' value for balancing time spent feeding and a reasonable chance of detecting danger. Here, then, are two clear and opposite predictions about *when* feeding and looking around for predators should occur and these can be distinguished by quantitative observations of the timing of these events. One hypothesis predicts random interscan intervals whatever the conditions, the other predicts non-random intervals, with a preferred peak that varies with conditions.

Beauchamp (2006) set out to test these predictions by observing the behaviour of wild flamingoes (*Phoenicopterus ruber ruber*) and recording the intervals between their scans. He used direct observation for limited sample periods each day, not all day watches or video, and so his study provides a beautiful example of how a well-designed but relatively simple set of observations can be used to distinguish two hypotheses when the right question is asked. Fig. 9.2 shows the views he had of flamingos feeding or being vigilant.

Flamingos are one of the species that Pulliam's hypothesis was supposed to cover. They feed by filtering water with their heads upside down under

Fig. 9.2 Views of flamingos feeding and looking up. Photographs by Guy Beauchamp.

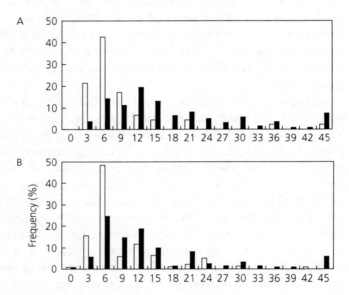

Fig. 9.3 Frequency distributions of interscan durations in flamingos foraging (A) during daytime and (B) on moonlit nights. Distributions are shown for small groups (one to five birds, open bars) and larger groups (more than five birds, black bars). In both cases there is a signficant depart-ure from a random distribution, although the precise conditions (e.g. large or small group size) also affect when and how often the birds scan. (From Beauchamp, 2006)

water, so they cannot look out for predators while they do so and they have to stop and look up from time to time. Using focal animal sampling and watching the birds for two relatively short periods during the day (15:30–17:00 and 18:55–21:00), Beauchamp recorded the times at which the birds put their heads in the water to feed and when they raised them to look around, as well as a number of other factors such as the size of the group they were in. His results showed that the times when the birds raised their heads were very non-random (Fig. 9.3). The mean intervals between one occasion when a bird looked up and the next depended on the size of group it was in, but within a group of a given size the intervals were much more constant than would be expected at random. The predictions from the Pulliam hypothesis were thus not upheld, and the simplest of observations were all that were needed to show that it did not explain observed behaviour, at least in this species.

9.2   When behaviour occurs: sequences

Intervals between events are an important way of establishing temporal connections as they are an indication that animals are responding either to what they themselves have done previously or to an external event, such as the behaviour of another animal or something else in the environment. A male bird calls, for example. Four seconds later, another calls. The closeness of these two events in time gives us the first clue that the call of one might be the stimulus for the other to call too. But stimuli do not always have such immediate effects. Perhaps we hear two birds calling, but the latency for one to respond is variable. Sometime it calls after 4 seconds but sometimes it waits 10, 20, or even 30 seconds before calling itself. Now we are less sure that one bird is acting as a stimulus for the other. Perhaps they both call and just happen to follow one another occasionally. Then we notice something else. The birds have several different calls. We can, in fact distinguish five or six different ones, perhaps more. And even if one male waits a variable time to respond to the other, we notice that he always chooses the same call as he has just heard to respond with himself. So even though the birds respond with a variable latency, the *sequence* of the calls is highly predictable. A powerful method of looking at connections between behavioral events that is not tied strictly to chronological time is to analyse sequence or order of behaviour, either the order in which one animal performs a sequence on its own or, even better, the order in which two animals produce sequences. This can produce clear evidence that the animals are acting as stimuli on each other and provide evidence of communication between them.

Hermit crabs (*Pagurus*) engage in fights, often about possession of a desirable shell. Instead of being covered all over with their own armour, like most crabs, hermit crabs have a naked abdomen and protect it by backing into an empty shell, such as a whelk or top shell. As the crab grows, it has to find bigger and bigger shells to live in, which is no problem as long as there are plenty of empty shells available. However, if the only shells around are already occupied by other crabs, hermit crabs will become extremely aggressive, even to the point of evicting the current occupant from the shell by violence

(Fig. 9.4). Crabs will repeatedly knock against the shell of the resident crab, attempt to prise it out, or engage in other acts of harassment (Dowds and Elwood, 1983). Sometimes the resident will just give up and crawl away, but sometimes overt fights can break out involving a number of different behaviours including claw waving, cheliped extension, and so on, but not necessarily at precise intervals. Hazlett and Bossert (1965) observed pairs of crabs to see if there was any evidence that these different behaviours occurred in particular sequences, as this would provide evidence that the behaviour of one crab was being influenced by what it saw the other one doing—the essence of 'communication'. By observing sequences of aggressive behaviour between crabs, they were able to show clear connections between the successive actions. Cheliped extension, in which the pointed ends of the claws are rapidly thrust towards the opponent, was much more likely to result in the opponent retreating than cheliped presentation, where the claw is held up and apparently shown to the opponent. Cheliped presentation appears to be a way in which two crabs assess each other's size before an actual fight (Elwood et al., 2006).

The analysis of intervals and sequences is now a complex subject, way beyond the scope of this book (Cox & Lewis, 1966; Slater, 1973; Haccou & Meelis, 1994) but the examples of the routine-loving chickens, the vigilant flamingos, and the aggressive crabs show how much can be learnt by simple recordings of time and order. Video and the other aids we will discuss in the next chapter are a great help in analysing time data but, as I hope these

Fig. 9.4 Hermit crabs will attempt to evict the occupants of desirable shells. Photograph by Bob Elwood

examples will show you, are not essential. Observational samples, based on scan sampling, focal animal sampling, or even opportunist behaviour sampling, can provide the raw material for doing perfectly valid studies about when behaviour occurs in relation to changing seasons, time of day, developmental age, the behaviour of the animals, and even the last time the animal performed the same or a different behaviour itself, and a host of other questions.

9.3   Where behaviour occurs

The same is true for the analysis of *where* animals are. You can use radio, GPS, and other tracking devices to collect huge amounts of data, and you can also use the comparably complex methods of analysis that have been evolved to deal with it (Chapter 10). For example, noting *where* animals are, tells us instantly a great deal about how they are responding to both features in their environment and to other members of their species. In many cases, it tells us where they have chosen to be and is, therefore, a very effective substitute for experimental tests on animal preferences in which animals are put into choice boxes in a laboratory (Dawkins, 2004). For example, instead of study-ing the food plant preferences of a small bird such as a goldfinch by catching it, putting it in an aviary, and then offering it what is probably an unnatural choice between different plants in pots, you study them in the wild and use where they choose to feed by themselves as their natural choice. If they have the freedom to go where they want, but you observe that they consistently choose only certain plants to feed from or certain bushes to roost, you have valuable information about their habitat preference, particularly if they cover a wide area and pass by other species. If you can measure habitat preference by comparing what is available to them to where the animals are actually found, that will be a much more convincing measure of choice than setting up artificial choices for them in a laboratory (Dawkins et al., 2003). And for some questions, such as the roosting preferences of starlings, or nest site selection in gulls, such *in situ* choices would be the only ones available. It would be impossible to set up a laboratory choice of nest or roosting sites.

Clutton-Brock et al. (1999) demonstrated the importance of measuring where animals do behaviour in their study of the sentinel behaviour of meerkats (*Suricata suricata*). Meerkats live in social groups and one animal will often stand on guard or sentinel duty while the others feed (Fig. 9.5). This behaviour was at one time thought to be altruistic—that is, the animals doing it appeared to benefit others while putting themselves at a disadvan-tage. While the rest of the group is feeding, one animal will climb up to a high point, such as a tree stump or a rock and keep watch. The sentinel does not

Fig. 9.5   Meerkat on sentinel duty while the rest of the group are feeding. Photograph by Helen L. Eaton

feed while it is on guard duty but it warns the others of the approach of danger. It therefore appears to be helping the other members of its group at some cost to itself: it is not taking the opportunities to feed that the others are enjoying and it is also apparently putting itself at risk.

To test the hypothesis that this apparently altruistic behaviour was in fact selfishly benefiting the sentinels themselves, Clutton-Brock et al. looked at where the sentinels positioned themselves in relation to the safety of a burrow. They found that sentinels tended to position themselves so that they were closer to a burrow than the animals that were feeding. This meant that sentinels tended to be the *first* to reach the safety of a burrow if a predator came. Certainly they warned the others but clearly not at the cost of putting themselves in more danger. Furthermore, the animals that went on guard duty turned out to be the ones that had recently been feeding and so were probably not very hungry anyway.

Observations on where and when the sentinels went on guard duty thus failed to reveal much in the way of altruism. The selfishly best strategy, the one that gives the individuals doing it the best chance of avoiding danger, is to go on guard duty when not hungry, stay near a bolt hole, and have the best chance of spotting the predator first and escaping down a burrow.

9.4   Tips and hints for recording where behaviour occurs

The simplest way of recording where animals are with respect to their environment is to use a *map* of the area the animals are occupying. The map could be anything from a published map of a whole area to a quick sketch map of a small area such as a field where you were observing the animals. If you draw your own maps, you can put in landmarks such as clumps of trees or water sources. If you photocopy them, you can them use one copy for each scan sample, noting the positions of animals or groups on each scan in relation to the landmarks. If you find it impossible to record the positions of all the animals quickly enough in each scan, you can simplify the map into areas, such as 'near the trees' or 'out in the open' and just count the numbers of animals in each of these areas (Dawkins et al., 2003). Even 'to the left of the fallen log' versus 'to the right of the fallen log' may, for some purposes, be enough. By surveying the area beforehand (or afterwards), you can make these crude maps more accurate by measuring out the distance between landmarks, and by placing these on your readymade maps you can plot where animals are more accurately.

For scan sampling, try to take your scans from the same place each time so that your observations (and their possible inaccuracies) are directly comparable. If you have to move around to see where all the animals are, always use the same path and try to take the same amount of time over the scan. You may also have to consider possible sources of inaccuracy in your observations, such as animals being hidden in the grass so you overlook them, being obscured by another animal, or affected by your own movements. General measurement error of this sort is almost inevitable, but make sure that you do not bias the results in favour of the prediction you are testing. For example, if you were testing the hypothesis that your animals would be in different places at different times of day and it was actually more difficult to see them at different times of day (perhaps because they lay down more), then you need to be careful that they really were in a different place, not in the same place but less visible.

A 'quick and dirty' but extremely useful method of recording where animals are with respect to each other, is to select a focal animal and then count the number of animals within one, two, or more body lengths of it

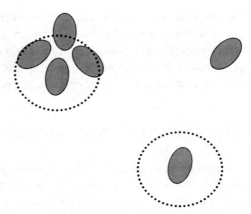

Fig. 9.6   Using the number of animals within a circle with a radius of a certain number of body lengths
gives an estimate of now many near neighbours an animal has. If you are using direct observation in the field, this circle can be an estimate (which should be validated against actual
measurements). If you are analysing photographs or video, the circle can be drawn on a sheet
of acetate placed over the image.

(Fig. 9.6). The advantage of using the animal's own body length rather than
real measurements is that you can 'measure' distance between animals,
regardless of their actual distance from you. There are no parallax problems
caused by the fact that the animals will appear to be smaller when they are
further away because a 'body length' will also be correspondingly smaller too.
This is even a good way of analysing video for the same reason. Instead of
worrying about the effects of camera distortion or the size of animals in different parts of the screen, just use the apparent body length of the animal in
the area of the screen you are interested in. Although this method sounds
crude and approximate, 'number of animals within one body length' of a
focal animal can be a very useful way of comparing how close together animals are under two circumstances, such as away from cover and close to
cover or in winter and in summer.

A useful variant of this method is to measure the *distance to nearest neighbour*. Ideally of course, nearest neighbour distances would be measured
more accurately than this (e.g. Clark & Evans, 1954; Febrer et al., 2006) but in
practice (when looking at a field of sheep, say, or troop of wild baboons),
ideal accurate measurements are not usually possible. By estimating how
close two animals are in terms of body size, you can quickly accumulate data
that allows you to detect changing patterns in where they are with respect to
one another (Lehner, 1996). Other ways of measuring social interactions
between animals by looking at their spatial relationships are described by
Arnold and Dudzinski, 1978; Stricklin et al., 1979; Arnold, 1985; Keeling and
Duncan, 1985, 1989; Ginsberg and Young, 1992; and Sibbald, et al., 2005.

9.5 Conclusions

The purpose of this chapter has been to give you a brief introduction to the range of different ways you can extend the basic observational samples—focal animal, scan, behaviour, and *ad libitum*—and use them to ask a range of different questions about behaviour. I have deliberately used examples employing 'traditional' methods (paper, maps, stop watches) because I wanted to show that you can still get a long way in the study of animal behaviour without expensive equipment. The right question and the right observations can still, even with all the technology that is now available, result in very good research with the bare minimum of aids. I also wanted to underline a point made throughout this book: that high-tech methods of recording behaviour give us the ability to measure and observe behaviour in ways that were previously only dreamt of, but they are not the solution to everything. What still matters most is the discipline of asking questions and collecting data in such a way that hypotheses are tested by comparing their predictions with what real animals do. But I am certainly not suggesting that you should turn your back on technology altogether. On the contrary, I hope that the experience of working without modern equipment will only make you appreciate its benefits even more. This discussion of the simpler methods of observing behaviour is therefore not a vote against technological aids to observation. It is in fact a preparation for the quite extraordinary observational revolution that is now breaking over our very heads.

10 Observing the future

'From time to time, one hears the claim that accurate studies of behavior can be made only in the laboratory, and that quantitative research on behavior is not practicable in the context of on-going, real-life situations. Such a restriction on research would mean that the behavioural sciences would forever forsake any hope of knowing whether their most powerful theories have any relevance to the world of behavior outside the laboratory. Unless we develop methods for field research that are comparable in sensitivity to those of the laboratory, the behavioural sciences will become progressively more isolated from the very behavior that their theories are supposed to explain.'

—J. Altmann (1974)

These words, written by Jeanne Altmann over 30 years ago, still need repeating today. Throughout this book, we have seen that observation is crucial to the study of animal behaviour and that it releases us, as it were, from the confines of the laboratory. We have seen that it allows us to ask questions about behaviour that might not even occur to someone whose only experience of behaviour was of what animals do in highly controlled and manipulated environments. We have also seen that it allows us to find answers to questions that apply in the real world and therefore to address problems that genuinely concern many people—problems in conservation, in animal welfare, and the many different ways in which humans interact with animals.

But the full power of observation is still not recognized even now and the observational approach is still seen as somehow inferior to experiment. I have heard research carried out on farms referred to as 'bucket science', with the obvious implication that it is not only muddy and messy but not very satisfactory either. 'Proper' science is still seen as clean, controlled and above all, experimental.

There are two very important points that this book has tried to make in response to this assumed superiority of experiment over observation. The first is that it is possible for there to be too much control, particularly in the field of behaviour, to the point that the results, although perfectly manipulated, lose their biological meaning. Dividing highly social animals into singletons or pairs and putting them in small cages to increase the number of replicates could, from a strictly statistical point of view, look like better science than observing them as a single group in a field. Independent replication is, after all, a cornerstone of good scientific procedure. But, as we have seen, the results of such a study could be worse than useless for showing anything interesting about the behaviour of the animals if, as a result of the splitting up of their social group, they were stressed and showed highly abnormal behaviour. Since many of the most interesting questions about behaviour are about what animals do when they are fending for themselves in the absence of humans and how they have evolved in their natural environments, an observational approach that keeps its distance and interferes as little as possible with the animals' lives, may often be the best or only way of answering them.

The second, and perhaps even more important point that has been a main theme of this book is that observational studies, if properly designed, can be just as scientific as experimental ones, but that the control that is exerted is the control of how the observer makes the observations, not over the animals themselves (Schneirla, 1950; Altmann, 1974). The same guiding principles for good experimental design—replication, not confounding variables, and reducing unwanted variation—also apply to good observational design. It's just that they are applied in somewhat different ways. For example, an experimenter might reduce unwanted variation by insisting that they would use nothing except animals of the same sex, the same genotype, the same age, and by making sure that their environments were so controlled that they all had identical diets and identical cages. An observer, on the other hand, might have no such control over the study animals, what ages or sexes they were, what their developmental histories had been, or even where the animals themselves chose to go on a particular day. But the results of a well-designed observational study do not have to reflect the havoc of all this uncontrolled and often uncontrollable variation. By using good design techniques, such as blocking (Chapter 4), the unwanted variation can be swept into known bundles (such as 'age', 'sex' etc) and put tidily to one side. It is still there, but because it has been collected in a controlled, designed way, it is known about and its effects on the main observations then eliminated statistically. It is literally 'part of the equation' (in this case the analysis of variance equation) and can be dealt with accordingly.

This 'taking what comes and dealing with it by good design' attitude that characterizes the observational approach has the further advantage that it roots any study to which it is applied very firmly in the real world. If, as an experimentalist, you have studied just one genotype, age, and sex of animal reared in a standard environment, then all you can draw conclusions about at the end of the study will be animals of that one genotype, age, sex, and rearing environment. But as an observer, unwrapping (in a statistical sense) those awkward sacks of unwanted variation, you already have valuable information about whether age, sex, and all the other variables do or do not have significant effects. Unwanted variance it might have been for the main question you were asking, but when collected in a disciplined way, such unwanted variance can turn into a veritable treasure trove of information. Having to 'make do' with a group of animals of many different ages and designing your study so that observations were blocked by age could tell you that age was (or was not) important, perhaps in addition to a main effects you were testing for.

Understanding how many different factors all interact is particularly important for studying animal behaviour, perhaps more so than in other areas of biology, because behaviour rarely has one single 'cause'. Behaviour is what animals finally do with all the cells and genes and nerves and muscles that make up their bodies. As such, it could be said to be the ultimate phenotype, the point at which what has been evolved meets and gets to grips with the world and either succeeds or fails. Eyes detect food. Ears hear a warning call. A brain 'decides' that, at that moment, eating the food is more important than flying away, and on that decision hangs life or death. Death might come from starvation or it might come from being eaten, and the decision of what to do next will depend on a range of factors from what other animals around it are doing to the signals from within the body about hunger level and the urgency of food. So many of the questions we ask about animal behaviour (Chapter 2) are about the animal's response to a complex and changing world. It is therefore in that complex and changing world that we need to study them. Observational techniques allow us to embrace and take account of this complexity. They give us the power, as Altmann recognized, to be in touch with the world outside the laboratory, where so many behavioural theories have to be tested and where so much behavioural research finds its relevance.

Why, then, does the importance of observation still have to be argued for? Why hasn't the long tradition of observation that was championed by Niko Tinbergen and Konrad Lorenz, and then given powerful support by the development of quantitative methods in the 1960s and 1970s by Cane (1961) J. Altmann (1974), Sackett (1978) and others, been enough to banish long ago the habit of that disparaging word 'mere' from regularly taking up a position next to the word 'observation'?

I think there is one basic explanation. This is that the full power of the observational approach has simply not been fully recognized because people have not realized that the same principles of good experimental design can be implemented just as rigorously with good observational design. Rightly concerned about good scientific procedure and rigorous testing of hypotheses, they have wrongly concluded that the control that is needed for 'good design' can only come from experiment and, more than that, from tightly controlled laboratory experiments where as many variables as possible are eliminated. They have not realized that control over how observations are made can go a long way towards substituting for control over animals and their environment. Then, convinced that only an experimental approach can lead to rigorous science, they have not thought it worthwhile to turn fully explore the full potential of observation.

While I hope that this book will have gone some way to dispelling these misunderstandings, I am also very hopeful that any lingering prejudices against an observational approach are about to be swept away by something that will completely change the way people think about observation in animal behaviour. We are, in fact, already undergoing an observational revolution. Observation is about to re-emerge centre stage in animal behaviour for one over-riding reason: technology.

You may have got the impression from reading this book that I was somehow against technology in the recording of behavioural data. The rather puritanical references to notebooks, paper, and pencils that occur in various places and the warnings against thinking that video recordings solve everything, could have been taken as my attempts to stop you from using anything other than the simplest means of recording your observations. The lack of emphasis could have suggested disapproval or even downright criticism. Nothing could be further from the truth.

The observational revolution we are now witnessing is only going to be possible because of technology, specifically because we can now record more information, and more different sorts of information about behaviour, than has ever been possible before. The sheer volume of information we can now record will demand, and indeed is already demanding, an emphasis on observational techniques as never before, this time reinforced with new techniques of statistical analysis. The ability we now have to track animals with satellite navigation and to know in every second in every minute in every hour where they are for days on end has led to new ways of analysing their home ranges, their interactions with each other, and how where they go relates to their food sources, ocean currents, and even minute details of topography. The photocopied maps we discussed in Chapter 6 are Stone Age technology compared to what is now available to answer questions about where animals are and with whom they interact.

Two examples will illustrate the possibilities of technology-enhanced observation. The first we encountered in Chapter 1. Douglas-Hamilton et al. (2005) followed individual African elephants using GPS trackers and found that what had previously been thought of as an elephants 'home range' was, as far as the elephants were concerned, not at all homogenous. There were some 'home sectors', usually protected areas, where the elephants moved slowly and spent a lot of their time, and these were linked by 'corridors' which the elephants used but always travelled through very quickly. This division of movement patterns into two distinct types showed that the animals had a quite detailed view of their range and even suggested that they an understanding that there was danger outside the protected areas. More recent studies have revealed the preferences elephants have for different routes, specifically routes that enable them to avoid going uphill (Wall et al., 2006). Tracks of elephants show that they systematically walk round hills rather than up them, even when the gradient is only slight and when their path takes them away from their preferred food. The explanation seems to be the huge energy costs for a large animal of climbing even the smallest hill. Wall et al. calculated that, for a 4 ton elephant, every 100 m climbed demands an extra 25 kcalories of food and this would take an elephant an additional 30 minutes of foraging time to find, over and above the 16–18 hours a day it spends feeding anyway. No wonder elephants are careful about hills.

GPS trackers can now be made small enough to be fitted to birds in flight (Fig. 10.1) and have, as our second example, been used to follow the paths taken by homing pigeons as they find their way back to their loft in much more detail than has ever been possible before. By plotting the path that has been taken by a pigeon onto a human map of the landscape it is flying over, it is possible to look for correlations between the pigeon's path and landmark features below it.

Fig. 10.1   GPS tracker fitted to the back of a homing pigeon that has just arrived back in its loft. Photograph by Dora Biro.

When this was first done, it looked as though pigeons were following linear features of the landscape such as roads, rivers, railway lines, field boundaries, and hedgerows (Guilford et al., 2004, Fig. 10.2). But perhaps the human eye was misled? Perhaps it was easier to pick out dramatic examples of pigeons following a main road and conveniently ignore the cases where

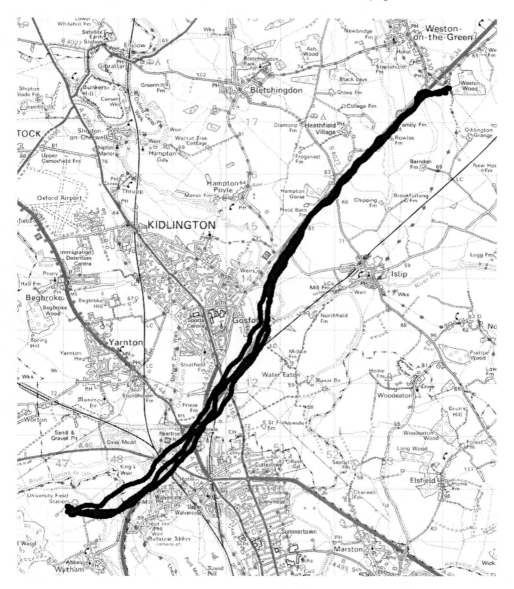

Fig. 10.2   Three GPS tracks of an individual pigeon released on three successive occasions from the same site (top right). The home loft is situated towards the bottom left of the map. Map courtesy Dora Biro.

tracks were unrelated to the landscape? Using statistical analyses more commonly used in engineering than in biology to define a 'linear feature', Lau et al. (2006) asked whether there were more such features in the landscape underneath the pigeon's chosen path than there were in adjacent 'control' areas. They found that there were. The pigeons were genuinely choosing to fly over regions with sharp straight edges and seemed to be attracted to linear features of the landscape. Once again, the 'control' here is not control over the animals, which were free to fly where they wished. The control is over what the researchers chose to do with the data obtained from those animals. Observation of how the animals were behaving naturally, aided in this case not just by technology but by imaginative use of statistics, has given a whole new insight into how (in a causal sense) pigeons find their way home. 'Mere' observation has truly come of age.

Webcams and CCTV now make continuous real-time recordings of behaviour not only possible but as easy as turning on a computer, so that it becomes clearer and clearer that the one thing we will not have to worry about in the future is scarcity of observational data. On the contrary, our problem is going to be how to analyse the vast quantities of data that are now available in such a way that we can make sense of it. My reason for emphasizing all along the 'pen and paper' approach is not to put you off using technology, but to prepare you for it. The glamour of having the most up to date equipment could blind you to the fact that the principles of good research design must still be applied to data collected with ease on a massive scale. It is still necessary to formulate precise research questions and to specify hypotheses and their predictions. It is still necessary to collect data in ways that fit the requirements of good research design even if the data is 'collected' after the event from video or other automated records. Choices still need to be made about what to select from the data stream, what to look for, how often and how long to sample for. In other words, understanding how to design simple pen-and paper observational studies is actually a very good preparation for dealing with the massive amounts of data that technology can now deliver. With any luck, it will help you not to lose your head and be seduced by all those vast streams of information. Perhaps, when confronted with what seems like all the data you could ever want, you will remember the lesson (Chapter 4) that in a house of 20,000 chickens, fitted with several video cameras all producing data for 24 hours and for 6 weeks on end, the problem may not be too much data but too little. If all those detailed records stacked up on your hard drive violate the principle of independence, for example, you may actually need to go out and collect more.

The technological advances that are fuelling the observational revolution should thus be seen as aids to what you would otherwise find impossible to observe or impossible to record, not research solutions in themselves. They enable you to observe for longer, or on more animals at once, or in places where the naked eye cannot follow. They are, or should be, your servants, your eyes and ears and hands, but not, in themselves, what makes you into a good observer of animal behaviour.

So, what does make a 'good observer'? It is now time to draw together the various elements that we have discussed in the course of this book into a synthesis of the path that all good observational research should follow. Indeed the questions you should ask yourself as an observer of animal behaviour are exactly the same questions that a good experimenter would also ask since, as we have seen repeatedly, observation, like any other kind of research, is a process of formulating and testing a hypothesis.

The questions that you need to answer are:

1. What *type* of question are you asking about behaviour? (Chapter 2)
   - About adaptation?
   - About what causes the behaviour?
   - About how behaviour develops?
   - About how the behaviour evolved?
2. What hypothesis are you testing? (Chapters 2 and 3)
3. What are the predictions from this hypothesis?
   - What would be the outcomes if the predictions are upheld?
   - What would be the outcomes if the predictions are not upheld?
4. How will you design your observations (Chapter 4) to ensure:
   - Independent replication?
   - That key variables are not confounded?
   - That unwanted variation is removed?
5. What have you selected (Chapter 5):
   - As your *level* of observation (group–individual–body part)?
   - As your *units* (behaviour patterns) to record?
   - For the type of *sampling* (focal animal, scan, *ad libitum*, behaviour)?
   - For the type of *record* (continuous, zero/one or something in between), with the consequent type *of measurement* (categorical, ranked or interval) that you will obtain?
6. How will you record behaviour? (Chapter 6) (paper, portable computer, CCTV, etc?)
7. Does your *protocol* (Chapter 6) specify:
   - The number of independent units (sample size)?
   - The number of observations from each independent unit?
   - Sample length and sample interval?
   - How animals will be chosen and/or identified?
   - The order in which observations will be made?
   - Other factors (e.g. weather, position on maps) that will be recorded?
   - Include a consideration of the *ethics* of your study?

8. Have you discussed the protocol with other people involved and obtained necessary permissions (Chapter 7)?
9. Have you done a pilot study to make sure everything is going to work?
10. What sort of statistical test will you do? (Chapter 8)

You may find it useful to use this list of questions in an iterative way—that is, to help you to design your research by letting the answers reveal some weakness which you then change as a result. For example, if you got down to question 8 and then realized that it was going to be impossible to record enough focal animal samples to achieve independence, you might have go back and rethink your whole design. The main point of the list is to help you troubleshoot your research plans *before* you spend all that time and effort doing research that turns out to be flawed.

But then, sitting once again on the harbour wall (oh yes, it does exist) I begin to wonder whether the checklist has not perhaps left out the most important element of all. This book was written in the belief that it was possible to help people to become better observers of animal behaviour by following a series of logical steps. I have no doubts at all that asking the right question is one of the most essential things to learn and that good design is critical to getting valid results. And I remain totally convinced that everyone should get into a statistical way of thinking even if they find the details of statistical tests a bit difficult to follow. But what is it about the eye and mind of the real observer that makes them stop in their tracks and notice that something an animal is doing is unusual or puzzling? Why is it that some people find animal behaviour so fascinating that they not only want to ask why an animal is behaving in the way that it is but are also prepared to spend time—possibly their whole lives—finding the answers. What makes someone want to become a good observer in the first place?

Distracted, I notice a large flock of gulls collecting in the harbour below me, the water about half way up their legs. They are standing, not feeding, and they have arrived just before the receding tide is about to expose the mudflats. This reminds me that there is one question I have singularly failed to answer throughout the entire book. Why do gulls foot-paddle? Mystery stories should have proper endings, so why (in any sense of the word) do they do it?

I shall now let you into a secret. We don't know. At least, we don't have the evidence that this book has argued that we have to have before we can be sure that we know. There are descriptions of the behaviour in gulls (Frieswijk, 1977; King, 1980), in ducks (Rogers, 1983), and even Little Grebes (Rolls, 1979), but all written over 25 years ago in a journal that is respected but not very widely read (*British Birds*). None of these papers is listed as having been subsequently cited by any other scientific authors and it therefore seems that no-one has studied foot-paddling much beyond the descriptive and speculation stages.

So why did I choose to begin and end this book with a behaviour that we don't understand? Wouldn't it have been better to take an apparently puzzling behaviour and then unravel it, piece by piece, to show how, with proper questioning and systematic observation, it shows itself to be entirely explicable? That would certainly have been a better course of action if my only motive in writing this book had been to show you how other people have observed animal behaviour and what answers they have found to their questions. But I had another motive, too, one that was not best served by emphasizing what other people have already done. I wanted to give you a sense of what there is yet to know about animal behaviour, of what we still don't know and—above all—of what you yourself might be able to discover.

Fig. 10.3   Photograph by Marian Stamp Dawkins.

REFERENCES

Allen, T. and Clarke, J. A. (2005) Social learning of food preferences by white-tailed ptarmigan chicks. *Animal Behaviour* **70**: 305–10.

Altmann, J. (1974) Observational study of behaviour: sampling methods. *Behaviour* **48**:1–41.

Altmann, S. A. (1968a) Sociobiology of rhesus monkeys. III. The basic communication network. *Behaviour* **32**: 17–32.

Altmann, S. A. (1968b) Sociobiology of rhesus monkeys. IV. Testing Mason's hypothesis of sex differences in affective behaviour. *Behaviour* **32**: 49–69.

Arnold, G. W. (1985) Associations and social behaviour. In: *Ethology of Farm Animals*. Ed. A. F. Fraser, pp. 233–46. Elsevier, Amsterdam.

Arnold, G. W. and Dudzinski, M. L. (1978) *Social Organisation and Animal Dispersion. Ethology of Free-Ranging Domestic Animals*. Elsevier, Amsterdam.

ASAB/ABS (2006) Guidelines for the treatment of animals in behavioural research and teaching. *Animal Behaviour* **71**: 245–53.

Beauchamp, G. (2006) Nonrandom patterns of vigilance in flocks of the greater flamingo, *Phoenicopterus ruber ruber*. *Animal Behaviour* **71**: 593–98.

Bednekoff, P. A. and Lima, S. L. (1998) Randomness, chaos and confusion in the study of anti-predator vigilance. *Trends in Ecology and Evolution* **13**: 284–87.

Berdoy, M. (1993) Defining bouts of behaviour: a three-process model. *Animal Behaviour* **46**: 387–96.

Boesch, C. (1991) Teaching among wild chimpanzees. *Animal Behaviour* **41**: 530–32.

Burley, N. (1988) Wild zebra finches have band-colour preferences. *Animal Behaviour* **36**: 1235–37.

Cane, V. (1961) Some ways of describing behaviour. In *Current Problems in Animal Behaviour* eds. W. H. Thorpe and O. L. Zangwill, pp 361–88. Cambridge University Press Cambridge UK.

Cheney, D. L. and Seyfarth, R. M. (1986) The recognition of social alliances among vervet monkeys. *Animal Behaviour* **34**:1722–31.

Cheney, D. L. and Seyfarth, R. M.(1990) *How Monkeys See the World*. University of Chicago Press, Chicago.

Clark, P. J. and Evans, F. C. (1954) Distance to nearest neighbor as a measure of spatial relationship in populations. *Ecology* **35**:445–53.

Clubb, R. and Mason, G. (2004) Pacing polar bears and stoical sheep: testing ecological and evolutionary hypotheses about animal welfare. *Animal Welfare* **13**: S33–40.

Clutton-Brock, T. H. and Albon, S. D. (1979) The roaring of red deer and the evolution of honest advertisement. *Behaviour* **69**: 145–70.

Clutton-Brock, T. H., O'Riain, M. J., Brotherton, P. N. M., Gaynor, D. Kausky, R. Griffin, A. S. and Mauser, M. (1999) Selfish sentinels in cooperative mammals. *Science* **284**: 1640–1644.

Couzin, I. D. and Krause, J. (2003) Effective leadership and decision-making in vertebrates. *Advances in the Study of Behavior* **32**: 1–75.

Cox, D. R. and Lewis, P. A.W. (1966) *The Statistical Analysis of Series of Events.* Methuen, London.

Creswell, W., Lind, J., Kaby, U., Quinn, J. L., and Jakobssen, S. (2003) Does an opportunistic predator preferentially attack nonvigilant prey? *Animal Behaviour* **66**: 643–48.

Crockett, C. (1991) Data collection in the zoo setting. In: *Wild Mammals in Captivity*, ed. S. Lumpkin and D. Kleiman. Chicago University Press, Chicago.

Cullen, E. (1957) Adaptations in the kittiwake to cliff-nesting. *Ibis* **99**: 275–302.

Dawkins, M. and Dawkins, R. (1969) Stochastic models of decision-making. In *Motivational Control Systems Analysis*, ed. D. J. McFarland, p 153, Academic Press, London and New York.

Dawkins, M. S. (1995) *Unravelling Animal Behaviour*. Longman, Harlow.

Dawkins, M. S., Cook, P. A., Whittingham, M. J., Mansell, K. A., and Harper, A. (2003) What makes free-range broilers range? *Animal Behaviour* **66**: 151–60.

Dawkins, M. S, Donnelly, C. A., and Jones, T. A. (2004) Chicken welfare is influence more by housing conditions than by stock density. *Nature* **427**: 342–344.

Dawkins, R. (1982) *The Extended Phenotype*. W. H. Freeman, Oxford and San Francisco.

Douglas-Hamilton, I., Krink, T., and Vollrath, F. (2005) Movements and corridors of African elephants in relation to protected areas. *Naturwissenschaften* **92**: 158–63.

Dowds, B. M. and Elwood, R.W. (1983) Shell wars: assessment strategies and the timing of decisions in hermit crab shell fights. *Behaviour* **85**: 1–24.

Dussutour, A., Deneubourg, J. L., and Fourcassie, V. (2005) Temporal organisation of bi-directional traffic in the ant Lasius niger (L.), *Journal of Experimental Biology* **208**: 2903–12.

Elgar, M. (1989) Predator vigilance and group size among mammals: a critical review of the evidence. *Biological Reviews* **64**: 13–34.

Elwood, R.W., Pothanikat, R. M. E., and Briffa, M. (2006) Honest and dishonest displays, motivational state and subsequent decisions in hermit crab shell fights. *Animal Behaviour* **72**: 853–59.

Emlen, S. T. and Wrege, P. H. (1989) A test of alternate hypotheses for helping behavior in white-fronted bee-eaters of Kenya. *Behavioral Ecology and Sociobiology* **25**: 303–19.

Engel, J. (1996) Choosing an appropriate sample interval for instantaneous sampling. *Behavioural Processes* **38**: 11–17.

Febrer, K., Jones, T. A., Donnelly, C. A., and Dawkins, M. S. (2006) Forced to crowd or choosing to cluster? Spatial distribution indicates social attraction in broiler chickens. *Animal Behaviour* **72**: 1291–1300.

Fisher, R. A. (1925) *Statistical Methods for Research Workers*. Oliver and Boyd, Edinburgh.

Fisher, R. A. (1935) *The Design of Experiments*. Oliver and Boyd, Edinburgh.

Fitzgibbon, C. D. and Fanshawe, J. H. (1988) Stotting in Thomson's gazelles: an honest signal of condition. *Behavioral Ecology and Sociobiology* **23**: 69–74.

Frieswijk, J. J. (1977) Black-headed gulls foot paddling on grassland. *British Birds* **70**(6):266–67.

Ginsberg, J. R. and Young, T. P. (1992) Measuring association between individuals or groups in behavioural studies. *Animal Behaviour* **44**: 377–79.

Goodall, J. (1968) *The Chimpanzees of Gombe*. Harvard University Press, Cambridge, Mass.

Gould, S. J. and Lewontin, R. C. (1979) The spandrels of San Marco and the Panglossian paradigm: a critique of the adaptationist programme. *Proceedings of the Royal Society of London B* **205**: 581–98.

Grafen, A. (1989) The phylogenetic regression. *Philosophical Transactions of the Royal Society of London* **326**:119–56.

Grafen, A. and Hails, R. (2002) *Modern Statistics for the Life Sciences*. Oxford University Press, Oxford.

Guilford, T., Roberts, S. J., Biro, D., and Rezek, I. (2004) Positional entropy during pigeon homing II: navigational interpretation of Bayesian latent state models. *Journal of Theoretical Biology* **227**: 25–38.

Haccou, P. and Meelis, E. (1994) *Statistical Analysis of Behavioral Data. An Approach Based on Time-Structured Models*. Oxford University Press, Oxford.

Harcourt, A. H., Harvey, P. H., Larson, S. G., and Short, R. V. (1981) Testis weight, body weight and breeding system in primates. *Nature* **293**: 155–57.

Harvey, P. H. and Pagel, M. D. (1991) *The Comparative Method in Evolutionary Biology*. Oxford University Press, Oxford.

Hazlett, B. A. and Bossert, W. H. (1965) A statistical analysis of the aggressive communication systems of some hermit crabs. *Animal Behaviour* **13**: 357–73.

Hosey, G. R. (1997) Behavioural research in zoos: academic perspectives. *Applied Animal Behavior Science* **51**:199–207.

Hrdy, S. B. (1974) Male-male competition and infanticide among langurs (Presbytis enetkkus) *Folia Primatologica* **22**(1):19–58.

Kamel, S. J. and Mrososvsky, N. (2005) Repeatability of nesting preferences in the hawksbill sea turtle, *Eretmochelys imbricata*, and their fitness consequences. *Animal Behaviour* **70**: 819–28.

Keeling, L. J. and Duncan, I. J. H. (1985) Some factors influencing spacing in domestic fowl in a semi-natural environment. In *Social Space for Domestic Animals*. Ed. R. Zayan, pp. 27–36 Martinus Nijhoff, Dordrecht.

Keeling, L. J. and Duncan, I. J.H. (1989) Inter-individual distances and orientation in laying hens housed in groups of three in two different enclosures. *Applied Animal Behaviour Science* **24**: 325–342.

King, B. (1980) Foot-paddling by pairs of herring-gulls. *British Birds* **73**: 312.

Kipling, R. (1902) *Just So Stories*. Reprinted (2000) in Penguin Classics series. Penguin, Harmondsworth.

Krause, J. and Ruxton, G. D. (2002) *Living in Groups*. Oxford University Press, Oxford.

Langton, S. D., Collett, D., and Sibly, R. M. (1995) Splitting behaviour into bouts: a maximum likelihood approach. *Behaviour* **132**:781–99.

Lau, K. K., Roberts, S. J., Biro, D., Freeman, R., Meade, J. and Guilford, T. C. (2006) An edge-detection approach to investigating pigeon navigation. *Journal Theoretical Biology* **239**: 71–78.

Lehner, P. N. (1996) *Handbook of Ethological Methods*, 2nd edition. Cambridge University Press, Cambridge.

Lorenz, K. (1958) The evolution of behavior. *Scientific American* **199**: 67–78.

Maddison, W. P. (2000) Testing character correlation using pairwise comparisons on a phylogeny. *Journal of Theoretical Biology* **202**: 195–204.

Martin, J. E. (2005) The effects of rearing conditions on grooming and play behaviour in captive chimpanzees. *Animal Welfare* **14**(2): 125–33.

Martin, P. and Bateson, P. P. G. (1993) *Measuring Behaviour. An Introductory Guide.* Cambridge University Press, Mass.

McCleery, R. H., Watt, T. A. and Hart, T. (2007) *Introduction to Statistics for Biology.* 3rd edition Chapman & Hall / CRC Boca Raton.

McKinney, F. (1965) The comfort movements of Anatidae. *Behaviour* **25**:120–220.

Meade, J., Biro, D., and Guilford, T. C. (2005) Homing pigeons develop local route stereotypy. *Proceedings of the Royal Society of London Series* B **272**: 17–23.

Moehlman, P. D. (1979) Jackal helpers and pup survival. *Nature* **277**: 382–83.

Pepperberg, I. M. (1999) *The Alex Studies: Cognitive and Communicative Abilities of Grey Parrots.* Harvard University Press.

Ploger, B. and Yasaukawa, K. (2003) *Exploring Animal Behavior in Laboratory and Field.* Academic Press, London.

Popper, K. (1959/2002) *The Logic of Scientific Discovery.* Routledge Classics.

Pulliam, H. R. (1973) On the advantages of flocking. *Journal of Theoretical Biology* **38**: 419–22.

Rogers, M. J. (1983) Foot-paddling by ring-necked ducks. *British Birds* **76**: 33.

Rolls, J. C. (1979) Foot paddling by pairs of herring gulls. *British Birds* **72**(4):184.

Rushen, J. (1991) Problems associated with the interpretation of physiological data in the assessment of animal welfare. *Applied Animal Behavior Science* **28**: 381–86

Russell, W. M. S. and Burch, R. L. (1959) *The Principles of Humane Experimental Technique.* Methuen, London.

Sackett, G. P. (1978). *Observing Behaviour. Vol. II Data Collection and Analysis Methods.* University Park Press, Baltimore.

Salmon, M., Wyneken, J., Fritz, E., and Lucas, M. (1992) Sea-finding by hatchling sea turtles—role of brightness, silhouette and beach slope as orientation cues. *Behaviour* **122**: 56–77.

Schneirla, T. C. (1950) The relationship between observation and experimentation in the field study of behavior. *Annals of the New York Academy of Sciences* **51**:1022–44.

Shepherdson, D. J., Mellen, J. D., and Hutchins, M. (1998) *Second Nature: Environmental Enrichment for Captive Animals.* Zoo and Aquarium and Biology and Conservation Series. Smithsonian Institution Press: Washington.

Shine, R. (1978) Propagule size and parental care: the 'safe habor' hypothesis. *Journal of Theoretical Biology* **75**: 417–424.

Short, R.V. (1979) Sexual selection and its component parts, somatic and genital selection, as illustrated by man and the great apes. *Advances in the Study of Behavior* **9**: 131–58.

Sibbald, A. M., Elston, D. A., Smith, D. J. F. and Erhard, H. W. (2005) A method for assessing the relative sociability of individuals within groups: an example with grazing sheep. *Applied Animal Behavior Science* **91**: 57–93.

Siegal, S. and Castellan, N. J. (1988) *Non-Parametric Statistics for the Behavioural Sciences*. McGraw-Hill, New York.

Slater, P. J. B. (1973) Describing sequences of behavior. Chapter 5 of *Perspectives in Ethology* Volume 1, ed. P. P. G. Bateson and P. H. Klopfer, pp. 131–153. Plenum Press, New York.

Smith, J. L. B. (1956) *Old Fourlegs—the Story of the Coelocanth*. Longman and Green, London.

Sokal, R. R. and Rohlf, F . J. (1969) *Biometry. The Principles and Practice of Statistics in Biological Research*. W. H. Freeman, San Francisco.

Stricklin, W. R., Graves, H. B., and Wilson, L. L. (1979) Some theoretical and observed relationships of fixed and portable spacing behavior of animals. *Applied Animal Ethology* **5**: 201–14.

Summers, K., McKeon, C. S., and Heying, H. (2006) The evolution of parental care and egg size: a comparative analysis in frogs. *Proceedings of the Royal Society of London B* **273**: 687–92.

Thomas, A. L. R., Taylor, G. K., Srygley, R. B., Nudds, R. L., and Bomphrey, R. J. (2004) Dragonfly flight: free-flight and tethered flow visualizations reveal a diverse array of unsteady lift generating mechanisms, controlled primarily via angle of attack. *Journal of Experimental Biology* **207**: 4299–4323.

Tinbergen, N. (1959) Comparative studies of the behaviour of gulls (Laridae): a progress report. *Behaviour* **15**: 1–70.

Tinbergen, N. (1963) On aims and methods of ethology. *Zeitschrift für Tierpsychologie* **20**: 410–33. (This journal is now called *Ethology*).

Tinbergen, N., Broekhuysen, G. J., Keekes, F., Houghton, J. C., Kruuk, H., and Szuk, E. (1962) Eggshell removal by the black-headed gull Larus ridibundus L: a behavioural component of camouflage. *Behaviour* **19**: 74–117.

Tolkamp, B. J. and Kyriazakis, I. (1999) To split behaviour into bouts, log-transform the intervals. *Animal Behaviour* **57**: 807–17.

Tyler, S. (1979) Time sampling: a matter of convention. *Animal Behaviour* **27**: 801–10.

Vogel, S., Ellington, C. P., and Kilgore, D. L. (1973) Wind-induced of the burrows of the prairie dog *Cynomys ludovicianus*. *Journal of Comparative Physiology* **85**: 1–14.

Wall, J., Douglas-Hamilton, I., and Vollrath, F. (2006) Elephants avoid costly mountaineering. *Current Biology* **16**: R527–529.

Watt, T. A. (1997) *Introductory Statistics for Biology Students*. 2nd ed. Chapman and Hall, London.

Weihs, D. (1975) Hydrodynamics of fish schooling. *Nature* **241**: 290–91.

Weir, A. S., Chappell, J., and Kacelnik, A. (2002) Shaping of hooks in New Caledonian crows. *Science* **297**: 981.

Whitehouse, A. M. and Hall-Martin, A. J. (2000) Elephants in the Addo Elephant National Park, South Africa; reconstruction of the population history. *Oryx* **34**: 46–55.

Appendix 1
Some random numbers

91011	09065	48503	26615
51426	22655	43980	09810
31006	84096	38289	66679
77468	87152	73799	48418
61029	20719	12647	40044
57108	25215	32049	65541
86411	04349	37937	41105
48809	54434	70106	89706
36698	72344	40829	40789
42453	93008	59547	00783
83061	83282	18547	71562
43769	31670	95493	34112
39948	63964	76895	46766
87031	55937	96395	31718
30767	21417	48302	45893
13953	49944	03180	96742
62098	38356	61486	43305
12825	98404	34183	99605
81744	14850	67803	13491
28882	17994	09243	29557
27369	17161	94822	24738
88183	98981	67749	83748
65846	31191	59799	25210
92545	75131	31093	62925

Appendix 2
Power and sample size

The power of a statistical test is the ability of a test to detect an effect, given that the effect genuinely exists. In other words, it is the probability that a test will reject the null hypothesis for a specified level of significance or 'p' value. In practice, one of the main ways of increasing statistical power is to increase the sample size, n. If the sample size is too small, there may be a genuine effect, but the test will fail to detect it (a Type II error).

You need to know/decide:

The significance level ('p'value). This is the probability of a Type I error—the probability that you have accepted that there was an effect when in fact there was no difference from the null hypothesis. A significance level of $p = $ or less than 0.05 is the largest value commonly accepted.

The power. This is 1-ß, where ß is the probability of a Type II error. Power = 0.80 is a common, if arbitrary value.

The effect size. A property of the differences between groups (Figure 6.1). The smaller the difference between groups, the more difficult it is to detect, and the larger your sample size will have to be.

Variation. Another property of the groups, usually measured as the standard deviation (sd) or the variance (V). This needs to be estimated from previous work or from your own pilot study.

Sample size: What you want to know. A rule of thumb is that he sample size $n = 4V/B^2$ where B is the error bound or confidence interval.

Most statistical packages will calculate required sample sizes for you. Alternatively, there is specialised software such as G*Power (www.psycho. uni-duesseldorf).

Appendix 3
Beaufort Wind Scale

Wind	Beaufort Number	Miles/hr	Km/hr	Effects
Calm	0	0	0	Smoke rises straight up
Light air	1	1–3	1–6	Smoke drifts slowly to show direction
Slight breeze	2	4–7	7–11	Wind felt on face; leaves rustle
Gentle breeze	3	8–12	12–19	Moves leaves and small twigs; extends light flag
Moderate breeze	4	13–18	20–29	Moves small branches;
Fresh breeze	5	19–24	30–39	Small trees sway; White caps on sea
Strong breeze	6	25–31	40–50	Large branches move; Hats blown off
Moderate gale	7	32–38	51–62	Whole trees in motion; Bow into wind to walk
Gale	8	39–46	63–75	Trees in violent motion
Strong gale	9	47–54	76–87	Shingles ripped off roofs; Small trees knocked over
Severe gale	10	55–63	88–102	Walls blown down; trees uprooted
Storm	11	64–75	103–119	Widespread structural damage
Hurricane	12	75+	119+	

INDEX

Lightning Source UK Ltd.
Milton Keynes UK
UKOW022135130113

204811UK00003B/8/P